INNER RIVAL

Silencing the Negativity Within

JEFF BUTORAC

Tremendous Leadership
PO Box 267 • Boiling Springs,
PA 17007 (717) 701 - 8159 • (800) 233 - 2665 •
www.TremendousLeadership.com

ISBN Paperback: 978-1-949033-87-8
ISBN ebook: 978-1-949033-88-5

DESIGNED & PRINTED IN THE

UNITED STATES OF AMERICA

TABLE OF CONTENTS

DEDICATION

I dedicate this book to my Mom and Dad, who always did everything they could to help us chase our dreams.

APPRECIATION

Every one of these people contributed to the creation of this book in some way, shape, or form. Thank you!

Mom and Dad, Eric, Maggie, Jack, Charlie, and Annie Butorac, Matt Eppen, Scott Reader, Bouthavy Khamratthanome, Tracey Jones, Michael Sherels, Doris Matter, Julie Jo Severson, Tim Schulte, David Lanza, Kim Mankey, Julie Rooke, Randy Wolfman, & George White.

INTRODUCTION

A boy and his grandfather are sitting by the fire one evening when the grandfather turns to the boy and says, "There is a battle going on inside all of us. It is a terrible fight between two wolves. One is evil – full of anger, jealousy, fear, greed, stress, and hate. The other is good – full of happiness, joy, empathy, patience, trust, caring, and compassion." The young boy thinks about this for a minute and then asks his grandfather, "Which wolf will win?" The grandfather replies, "The one you feed."

This passage had a massive impact on me. I first read it when I was going through a difficult time in my life, struggling with the negative voice inside my head. The thing about negative thinking is that it slowly trickles into your mind and takes control. Oftentimes, you don't even realize when it's happening. This can be especially true when it comes to competitive sports and other types of performances. My Inner Rival took center stage at multiple points of my life, including my time as a high school and college athlete and my twelve-year basketball coaching career.

When my Inner Rival surfaced, I allowed my mistakes and disappointments on the court to overshadow everything I enjoy about sports– building relationships with the people around me, working with athletes as they build new skills, and being in a competitive environment. I lost sight of these joys because I didn't have the tools to combat the negative voice as it would arise. Eventually, all that negative energy trapped within my mind and body led to so much anxiety that I couldn't force myself to leave the house, let alone walk into a gym to coach my team.

Rock bottom finally came when the panic attack hit, and I wasn't able to leave the house for work. My hands were shaking, and my heart was racing. My mind was going a million miles a minute while at the same time feeling depleted. I didn't know where to go or what to do. I knew something had to change and fast!

After twelve years chasing my dream of becoming a head basketball coach, my career came to a screeching halt. I had to quit for mental health reasons. I was devastated, confused, and nervous. I knew I couldn't go on any longer feeling like this. I needed to get myself right mentally. But how? I had already tried everything I could think of. Nothing seemed to reduce my levels of anxiety or panic.

This book grew out of a desperate need for inner calm, direction, and a desire to silence the negative voice in my head. The good news is that in time, through years of self-reflection, study, and hard work, I made a transformative realization. I realized that I have the ability to choose my mindset and control the voice in my head. I knew it would not magically happen. I needed to put in the work. So, I set out on a mission to learn how to combat the doubts, disappointments, fears, and anxiety that were bombarding my brain every day. I quickly began to see and feel the changes in my life.

My hope in writing this book is to help you see past your perceived limitations and unleash your courage to move toward the future you aspire to create. I hope to help you understand there is always a way past the challenges and obstacles you run into along the way. Lastly, I hope to help you stay aware of and silence your Inner Rival—that negative voice that will always be there trying to pull you down.

How I Got Here

I grew up in Rochester, Minnesota, a 100,000-person town in the southeastern part of the state that is most notably known for the world-famous Mayo Clinic. I was part of a sports-loving family with two fantastic parents who raised us to work hard while never overdoing their involvement with our sports. Growing up, my brother and I played every sport that we could. We loved traveling and competing at different levels throughout our youth. My childhood was filled with making friends, hanging out in hotels, and experiencing the excitement of competition and playing in tournaments. Those were some of my favorite memories from growing up. I couldn't have asked for a better childhood and more supportive family.

Throughout my entire life, my parents have owned and operated the local tennis club. It has a family friendly, *Cheers*-like atmosphere, "where everybody knows your name." It was my daycare, a second home, a place to hang out, and where I gained my first work experiences. I loved the community, fitness, and fun of that environment. It was a place that I could feel comfortable being myself and learn to grow as a person and in athletics.

To say tennis was a big part of my family would be an understatement. Both my dad and older brother were national champions in tennis at the collegiate level. My brother went on to participate at the highest level in the ATP Tour and in tournaments like Wimbledon and the US Open. I couldn't have been prouder of my brother and everything that he achieved. Because of him, I had the opportunity to travel around the world and observe the life of professional athletes: the way they train, prepare, compete, socialize, and spend free time.

Jealousy of my brother's success was never an issue for me. I say this because if you had seen my behavior on the tennis court, you would have thought I was fighting a demon, which I was. But the demon wasn't envy and it wasn't any sort of unrealistic expectation set by my parents. It was that I had no idea how to control my emotions and mindset while making mistakes on the court. I would let my immediate emotions get the best of me and take control of my actions. That is rarely a good idea.

Showing negative emotion on the court is often frowned upon in the tennis culture. That is one of the elements that makes the sport so challenging. Controlling those negative emotions can be extremely difficult, especially when you are on your own trying to figure out how to beat your opponent. I personally believe that tennis is the most isolating sport there is. There are no teammates or a coach to talk to during a match if things aren't going well. In team sports, if you're playing poorly, you can lean on your associates for help and also find different ways to contribute to the team's success. Even in boxing you may retreat to a corner and coach after each round. Tennis provides neither a place to hide nor a person on which to lean (unless you are playing doubles). You are on a stage all by yourself and the success and failure are yours alone to bear.

Before I learned tools to better handle my missteps and failures more gracefully, I had a bad habit of throwing my racket and spewing four-letter words. My behavior was embarrassing. It was an instant reaction that I couldn't figure out how to control (missed easy shot equaled racket throw). Deep down, I knew I didn't want to act that way. But I couldn't figure out how to control myself enough to stop. As a result, I stepped away from tennis during my junior year of college.

Tennis wasn't the only sport I played. As much as I enjoyed tennis, I *loved* basketball. I played until my junior year of high school and loved being with the guys. Whether I'm playing or coaching, there's something magical about walking into a full gym on a Friday night with the crowd buzzing, the band playing, the smell of popcorn wafting in the air, and a group of five guys on the court playing in sync. I knew that's where my heart was.

After I graduated from Saint John's University (SJU) in Collegeville, Minnesota, in the spring of 2007, I decided to give everything I had to becoming a college basketball coach. My parents knew the coaching profession would require long and hard hours for very little money in the beginning, and they were gracious enough to help me on this journey by showing strong support and helping me financially. Because of them, my dream became a reality.

My first coaching position was with the University of Wisconsin-Eau Claire (UWEC) men's basketball team. For two years I worked as their second assistant. I quickly realized although I knew how to *play* basketball, I had no idea how to *coach* it. I was lucky enough to work with another assistant coach who took me under his wing. It soon became an obsession to learn everything I could about helping players unlock their potential and maximize their performance

I watched instructional movies and game films, talked with other coaches about strategies, and read hundreds of books by coaches and experts on leadership, communication, and teamwork. Because I hadn't actually played college basketball, I always felt that I needed to prove myself and my knowledge of the game. I was extremely motivated to do so. But that is when my ego got involved and anxiety began to show its ugly face.

The profession of college coaching can be a journeyman lifestyle and at times feel a bit isolating. Coaches often change positions every year or two as they work their way up the coaching ladder at different schools. I was no different. I spent two years at UWEC. I then went back to my alma mater, SJU, to be an assistant varsity coach and junior varsity head coach. It was a fun opportunity to get back to a school I love and be part of a successful and historic program.

I spent one year at SJU and decided I no longer wanted financial help from my parents. My plan was to move to Saint Paul, get a "real job," and be a high school coach on the side. I was extremely lucky to join a great program and spent four years coaching basketball at Burnsville High School with three guys who would basically become my brothers. We experienced both enjoyable and difficult times as a group. Still, today, we have a brotherhood that will last a lifetime. But it still felt like something was missing from my coaching career. So, I took another leap.

I received an offer to be a graduate assistant coach at a school I had never heard of in a state to which I had never been. I packed a trailer and headed down to Southern Arkansas University, in the city of Magnolia, to coach women's college basketball for two years. This was my first real experience with culture shock. It was one of the few counties in the country that was still dry. That means no bars or nightlife. I'm not a big drinker, but I was a single, 30-year-old guy who didn't know anyone in that town of only ten thousand people. The lack of social opportunities became more than just a little bit isolating.

While living and coaching in Arkansas, I earned my Master of Science degree in kinesiology and coaching. I ended up making a few good friends but as soon as my time was up, I left. I couldn't wait to get back to some type of familiar civilization. I took the first exciting job that came my way, which was a position as head boys' basketball coach at Century High School in my hometown.

I was ecstatic and nervous for the opportunity to run my own program. I couldn't wait to build a dynasty with the knowledge I had accrued over the previous 9 years.

That's when the anxiety began to get severe…

Anyone who has ever been a head coach at the college or high school level knows that the job is about 30 percent actual coaching. The rest is tending to administrative work, talking to parents, and putting out fires. We must also deal with emotional highs and lows on an almost daily basis. If you don't understand how to regulate and work with those emotions, they can quickly drain your energy and distract you. That's exactly what happened to me.

I had trouble letting go of the mistakes and losses and an even tougher time finding enjoyment in the improvements and wins. I knew there were positives to take away from the job, such as the coaching staff I was working with, spending time with the players, and the enjoyment of being in a competitive environment. But I didn't have the tools to level myself out mentally and lost sight of why I enjoyed coaching the game in the first place.

This ruminating on negative emotions got worse and began to spill over into my life outside of basketball. I became distant from friends and family and was rarely in a good mood when I was around them. Since I couldn't get my mind to slow down and separate basketball from the rest of my life, I began avoiding social situations. I reacted more emotionally to everything every day, and then beat myself up for feeling that way. I took every comment personally and was catastrophizing situations constantly. I knew I was in a rough spot.

One day, the anxiety became so bad that I couldn't make myself leave the house to go to work, let alone walk to the gym to coach my team. As soon as the season finished, I had to step away from coaching basketball for mental health reasons. I was devastated, confused, and nervous. After twelve years of chasing my dream of becoming a head basketball coach, I had to quit.

I knew I needed to get myself right mentally. After much persuading from my family, I began by meeting with a counselor who guided me toward a more productive path of thinking. Then I dug in and did the work by consuming every resource on mental toughness I could find. I read books about willpower, confidence, and resilience. I watched videos, highlighting the mindset of US Navy SEALs and other Special Military Operations. I read stories about people who overcame excruciating challenges with mental fortitude and resilience. These stories included ultramarathon runner David Goggins, Holocaust survivor Victor Frankl, basketball player Kobe Bryant, and US Navy SEAL Marcus Luttrell.

With time and effort, I have been able to strengthen my mindset and emotional stamina, resulting in more inner calm and resolve. I have come to realize mental toughness is the most important quality for success in sports and life. Without it, you will never be able to unlock all the physical and mental gifts that you have inside. It determines your effort, discipline, focus, enjoyment of life, confidence, and achievement of everything you hope for.

Since I stepped away from coaching basketball, I have mentally stepped into a much better place! I have been able to strengthen my mindset, confidence, and ability to handle adversity to a point that I had never reached before. I am now able to focus my mindset more on what I can control and ignore the things I cannot control. It wasn't easy. It took days, weeks, months, and even years of doing the difficult work of looking at myself, my thoughts, beliefs, and actions. But I couldn't be happier to be where I am mentally with my ability to silence my Inner Rival.

There are still days and situations that can be difficult for me, either mentally, physically or emotionally. But by using the tools featured in the following chapters, I can turn down the negative voice in my head and turn it into something positive much sooner.

My New Mission

My mission now is to help you! I'm excited to share what I've learned and used in my own life to create a champion's mindset and silence your Inner Rival. Together, we will build a toolbox that will prepare you for whatever battles are ahead in your life. The tools outlined in this book are helpful for athletes, coaches, performers, and anyone else looking for more inner calm and strength. It doesn't matter if you want to be a better fireman, mom, salesperson, business owner, coach, or just physically and mentally fit. These tools will help you direct your focus where it will be beneficial to you and keep you moving forward. To this day, I still battle with my Inner Rival, but the more I use these tools, the quieter my Inner Rival becomes.

As a coach, I've always believed sports are a fantastic way to teach athletes lessons for life outside of sports. I still feel that way today. The great part about these tools is they can help you in any situation, whether sports related or not. You can use them to overcome fears, have difficult conversations, and work through physical or mental obstacles. No matter your plight, these tools will help!

Applying the following tools won't necessarily be easy. And that's okay. Nothing worthwhile in life is ever easy. Their integration into your daily routine will require self-check-ins and continued self-awareness, which can be uncomfortable. There have been times I have had to come to some hard truths with myself and really examine whether my actions reflect what is important. It's going to take time and effort. But I have no doubt that you will see and feel the benefit of your work.

You won't wake up one day and suddenly feel mentally tough. It's a daily process. It means facing challenges, not giving up, and finding a way to move toward your goals and making pivots when necessary. It means understanding that you will get knocked down, but you will choose to get up. It's a lifestyle.

Your Inner Rival will always be there. The voice has the knack for getting louder at the most critical moments of your journey, so you want to be sure to have the tools to be able to silence it when inner strength is needed most.

All of my discussion about mental toughness includes emotional control as well. They're intertwined. It is nearly impossible to work on one without influencing the other.

What is Your Inner Rival?

Your Inner Rival is that voice in your head creating doubts, fears, stress, and anxiety. It's the voice trying to convince you that you're not good enough, smart enough, or motivated enough. The voice plants the seed of doubt in your thoughts right before you attempt the big shot. The voice causes you to freeze when giving a presentation. The voice whispering, "You don't have what it takes to achieve your dream." We all have an Inner Rival. It will always be there, but you don't have to listen to it.

University of Michigan Head Football Coach Jim Harbaugh describes the Inner Rival voice as a fictional character he made up named Freddie P. Soft:

> "He's a four-inch guy that wears a cape and a hat with a plume in it. And he's just tall enough to talk right into your ear and tells you, 'You don't have to practice today,' 'Why are you working so hard?' or 'Get over there in the shade. There's no need to attack with enthusiasm today. So, take a break. Take a knee.' Yeah, he's a not a guy you want around. You want to get him off your back as soon as possible".[1]

As nomads and hunter-gatherers, our ancestors had to develop the fight or flight response in their brains to survive threats of wild animals and the environment. When we perceive a threat, our brains' limbic system, specifically the amygdala, responds in a split second by activating the sympathetic nervous system. As a result, our body releases hormones that can cause the heart rate to increase, breathing to accelerate, blood pressure to rise, and pupils to dilate. These natural responses served as warnings to hunters to handle threats to stay alive. Although most of us don't have those same types of threats today, our brains still act in a similar fashion.

Instead of a wild animal, the threat ahead of us today may be more along the lines of making a game-winning shot, giving a presentation at work, dealing with a difficult boss or coworker, walking into a new social setting, or preparing for a big test. Our bodies go into fight or flight mode. Without the right kind of mental discipline, our Inner Rival can easily sway us to flee toward those familiar negative thoughts, which make us feel safe despite their negativity. With practice and awareness, you can use those thoughts, emotions, and bodily changes to your advantage.

There are countless examples of the Inner Rival rearing its ugly head for athletes and performers. Steve Sax is a former Major League Baseball player who played for several teams but started his career with the Los Angeles Dodgers in 1981. After having an amazing first year he won the Rookie of the Year award in 1982. The following year didn't go as well. He committed 26 errors by the All-Star break. But even worse than that, he found himself unable to throw the short toss from second base to first. He experienced a classic example of the "yips." The yips occurs when an action that is usually common and easy for that sport becomes uncommonly difficult. Steve Sax provides a perfect example of someone who endured a nasty bout with their Inner Rival!

During the 1983 All-Star break, Sax visited his father, who would soon after pass away. His father explained Sax suffered confidence issues instead of a mental block. His father implored him to continue to work hard in practice and not give up in order to regain his confidence. Steve listened to his father. He continued to stay focused and work hard in practice. He regained his confidence quickly and began getting his career back on the right path. By 1989 he had the highest fielding percentage (.987) among second basemen in the entire MLB.

I personally had a nasty case of the yips for a short period in my life. In high school, college and for years after I was a teaching pro at my parents' tennis club. After so many years of playing and teaching tennis, hitting a tennis ball to people that want to learn becomes extremely easy. I could almost put it on the player's racket. That was true until I experienced the yips.

I stepped out on the court one day and completely forgot how to feed a tennis ball. I would feed one into the net, and the next would be 10 feet out. After that I would put it 5 feet wide of the student, with the next ball going five feet wide in the other direction. I couldn't figure out what was going on! I completely forgot how to feed a tennis ball! It was as if I was a beginner all over again.

This persisted for about a year or two. To say that it was embarrassing would be an understatement. I was a former college tennis player struggling to feed the tennis ball to people just learning the game. I had no confidence in myself on the court.

How did I get out of it? Just like Steve Sax. I practiced until I couldn't get it wrong. Once I managed to make good feeds for a lesson or two, my confidence came back. The yips went away and I haven't had to deal with them since. But that was neither the first nor the last bout I would have with my Inner Rival.

In the world of sports and performers there are also many great examples of people silencing their Inner Rivals and being able to choose their mindset. Two of them are National Football League quarterbacks Patrick Mahomes of the Kansas City Chiefs and Josh Allen of the Buffalo Bills. In the 2022 AFC Championship game they both put on a magical performance that will go down in history.

With 1:54 left in the game, Josh Allen threw for a touchdown to go up 29-26. In football, usually having two minutes or less left in a game to score a touchdown is difficult, but that day would be different. After getting the ball down 3 points with 1:54 left in the game, Mahomes drove the Chiefs down and scored a touchdown to take the lead 33-29 with just 1:02 left on the clock. Allen, not to be outdone, got the ball and quickly drove down to score a touchdown and take the lead 36-33 with just 0:13 seconds left on the clock! With Mahomes being who he is, that was just enough time for him to make some magic happen, which he did! In just 0:13 seconds he was able to get the team in position to kick the game-tying field goal with no time left on the clock.

In overtime, the Chiefs got the ball first and quickly drove down to score a touchdown one more time and win the game.

It was amazing to witness how these two players were able to silence their Inner Rivals with so much on the line. Neither one of them flinched! It all came down to who had the ball last. Those two were picture-perfect examples of someone being able to silence their Inner Rival in the most difficult of situations.

Silencing Your Inner Rival

It's time to silence your Inner Rival. Your Inner Rival is holding you back from unlocking your greatness. You have the freedom of choice to combat it. With this book, I aim to help you quiet that voice that turns challenging situations into perceived threats, such as preparing for a big race, getting healthy and fit, facing a difficult opponent, or taking on a task that you've never done before. You will learn the tools to embrace the challenges of life and focus more on what's in your control. Then, those perceived threats will turn into mere obstacles that you're able to overcome.

Silencing your Inner Rival isn't about turning off your feelings and becoming emotionless. Emotions are great! They give life meaning. But most of the bad decisions we have made throughout our lives happen when our emotions take control of our decision making.

I want to help you to embrace the emotions you feel, but not to let them take over the way you think. Each chapter in this book introduces a different method for improving your mental strength and emotional stamina. You'll learn how to use your body's natural biological responses to your advantage. You'll learn how to keep your self-talk positive and productive, as well as how to notice when it's turning negative. You'll learn ways to push yourself past your perceived limits and take command of your focus and discipline. You'll gain visualization and meditation techniques to improve brain functions.

Each tool or method will enhance the others. The more of them you adopt into your daily routine, the stronger the others will become.

I use every single tool outlined in this book for myself and the athletes and performers I mentor. I sincerely hope by working through the exercises at the end of each chapter, you'll grow in your emotional resilience and strengthen your mindset. Your Inner Rival is by far the most difficult opponent you'll ever face. It knows your biggest fears and attacks when you least expect it. Together, we'll make sure you have the tools to Silence your Inner Rival when it bares its ugly teeth.

Chapter 1

GOAL SETTING

"A goal without a plan is just a wish."
—Antoine de Saint-Exupery

Inner Rival

Goal setting is an important step in building your mental toughness and quieting your Inner Rival. Without a goal you truly believe in and care about, you're going to find it difficult to push yourself and stay disciplined in the face of challenges and adversity. Your Inner Rival tries to convince you that you've done enough and don't need to work any harder. It distracts you from your goal and diverts your attention. By creating a goal with awareness and intention, you'll give yourself a North Star to guide you toward success.

Introduction

One of the best ways to get from where you are to where you want to be is by setting goals that you're passionate about. But why, then, do up to 43 percent of people who set New Year's resolutions give up by February? There may be any number of reasons, including:

- Expectations are too high or not realistic.
- They have no plan to achieve results.
- They lack motivation.

These are the ploys of the Inner Rival that keep you from reaching your potential. By learning how to set goals productively, you remove your Inner Rival's power to trip you up with obstacles that seem too difficult to overcome.

Goal setting is a skill, and there is a strategy for sharpening it. In this chapter, you'll learn to build your own blueprint for achieving excellence, using the goal setting tools I use to help athletes every day. You can also use this method for other areas of your life. Creating a quality plan takes time and effort but achieving a goal that is meaningful—while keeping the Inner Rival at bay—is well worth the extra work.

Why Set Goals?

Goal setting is one of the most frequently used tools by US Olympic athletes and coaches. It's said to be "arguably the most effective performance enhancement technique in the behavioral sciences".[2]

Before I dive too far into the goal setting process, here are some of the advantages of the plan we're going to create together to achieve your goals. The plan will:

- Keep you on target and focus your attention.
- Increase confidence as you achieve your stepping-stones.
- Help you defeat the fear of failure and gain resilience.
- Improve time management.
- Strengthen willpower and discipline.
- Help to foster strategy in overcoming challenges.

In a compilation of over 500 scientific studies about goal setting in different fields, two key findings appeared. First, difficult goals produce higher levels of performance than easy ones. Secondly, goals set with more specific guidelines are more effective than vague ones or no guidelines at all.

An example from one of the studies shows how goal setting benefits athletes, even at the highest level:
In 1983, Damon Burton completed his doctoral dissertation by putting the Goal-Setting Training (GST) program to the test. GST was designed to teach athletes to set appropriate performance goals. He worked with the University of Illinois swim team for an entire season, from the first day of practice until the end of the last meet. He systematically taught the women's team, the men's team and the swim coach the principles of setting goals. Burton's study made two comparisons. He compared the Illinois swimmers who became skilled at establishing defined, accurate (only a small difference between their pre-race goal and actual time), and realistic goals with teammates who did not become skilled at setting quality goals. He made the same comparison with the Indiana University swim team, which was a perennial powerhouse in the Big Ten Conference and the nation. The Indiana team did not receive the GST program.

Both comparisons in the study showed, in general, that athletes who became quality goal setters by participating in the GST program:

- Were more focused
- Were more self-confident

- Performed better
- Were more satisfied with their participation.[3]

These results show the many benefits to setting goals, when done correctly, even at the highest levels of athletics. It doesn't end with athletics. The growth and development resulting from goal setting in sports can be applied to any situation: work, relationships, or health and fitness.

Long-term Versus Short-term Goals

Long-term goal setting and short-term goal setting both have their strengths and are most effective when used together. One without the other can create a lack of motivation and make it more difficult to reach your final destination. Short-term goals keep you in motion and celebrating success, while the long-term goal directs your trajectory towards your final destination.

When creating a long-term goal, choose something you're genuinely passionate about. To be an effective long-term goal, choose one YOU want to achieve and not one somebody else sets for you. If it's not something you sincerely want to accomplish, it is more difficult to stay motivated over the long haul.

Staying motivated can often be easier when focusing on short-term goals and daily tasks than it is to stay motivated and focused on a long-term goal. It's important not to spend too much time focusing on your long-term goal, because it may take a lengthy amount of time before you achieve it, and for some, motivation can be difficult to maintain over an extended period of time. Procrastination and laziness can creep their way in when a goal is in the distant future. Instead, put your focus on your short-term goals. They don't take as long to achieve, and each time you complete one, you gain confidence and motivation for progressing to the next one.

What are short-term goals? They are the stepping-stones toward the final outcome you hope to achieve. They're the goals you'll meet daily, weekly, or monthly during the process of reaching the long-term goal. They are what should receive most of your focus because they take you to the finish line. These goals are your "how-to process" to achieve your outcome. And, as most coaches will tell you, it's more important to focus on the process than the outcome.

Easy Goals vs. Challenging Goals

If you are new to setting goals or to a subject area, it can be a bit difficult at first to choose between an easy goal and a challenging goal. It may take a little trial and error to figure it out. Stay persistent. When you set goals that are clear and slightly challenging, rather than setting a goal that is vague, too easy, or extremely difficult, you will see more success and growth.

Now, this isn't an exact science, so every person will be a bit different. Some people thrive when they have extremely challenging goals in front of them, while others become overwhelmed by the getting pushed far outside of their comfort zone and need to set smaller, easier goals along their path. It is important to figure out what kind of goal person you are and set those consistently to stimulate your growth and improvement. Most people that set challenging goals will find they excel more than if they had set easy goals.

The Three Types of Goals

The type of goal you establish can have a massive influence on your mindset, your motivation level, and likelihood of achieving it. Making sure you are setting the correct type of goals is a pivotal step and can be a determining factor in whether you're successful or not.

Outcome Goals

The most common goal type is an outcome goal. It's exactly as it sounds. You're setting a goal to achieve a particular outcome. It could be anything from winning a game or making the team, to making the sale or achieving a certain weight. These are great goals to set, but they have their flaws if you concentrate on only the outcome and not what it takes to get there.

The outcome goal is usually influenced the most by outside sources. You have the least control over that type of goal and whether or not it is achieved. You might do everything within your control and play a perfect game, but because of an unlucky bounce, injury, or call by a referee, you don't win. The loss doesn't mean you didn't do your best. It just means that outcome goals have many factors out of your control that influence the final result. While it's good to set an outcome goal, it's best not to spend too much time focusing on it.

Performance Goals

Performance goals can be advantageous to set on your way to pursuing your outcome goal because you have more control over your success than you do with the final outcome. Examples of performance goals would be shooting 90 percent from the free throw line, running a marathon at an eight-minute-mile pace, or writing one blog a week for a year. By setting these types of goals, you'll be more focused on your personal performance rather than basing your success solely on wins, losses, or the outcome. If you meet your performance goals, then the outcome goals will be more attainable.

An example of how Outcome and Performance goal types can work in sync:

The outcome goal of the basketball team is to win the conference title. The coach believes that the best way to win games is to out rebound the opponents. Getting more rebounds than the opponents thus become the performance goal. By focusing on getting more rebounds than their opponents, they hope to win the conference title. This strategy helps by putting more focus and energy on something over which they have more control (getting rebounds). If they outre-bound opponents, but still fail to win games, they can shift their focus toward a different performance goal that will be more beneficial to their journey of reaching their outcome goal.

Process Goals

I believe process goals are the most important types of goals to set. They define your "process" for achieving your other goals. You should set at least one, if not multiple, process goals on the way to achieving either your performance goal and/or your outcome goal. Examples of process goals would be shooting one hundred free throws at the end of practice, going to the batting cage three days a week in the off-season, or getting to the office 30 minutes early every day to get small tasks done. These are goals that are nearly 100 percent within your control. They are daily stepping-stones (short term goals) toward your larger goals. Process goals are the most important ones you can set as you almost completely control them.

A process goal is a great way to build self-confidence. By setting goals within your control and completing them, you're witnessing discipline, focus, and success. The biggest contributor to the feeling of self-confidence is previous success. The more success you achieve, the more confident you'll feel in that skill or situation. This new confidence will move you toward the next, perhaps more difficult, process goal.

Nick Saban is arguably the greatest NCAA Football Coach of all-time with seven National Championships. One of the things that makes him a great coach is his coaching philosophy, which he calls "The Process." He describes it as follows.

"Well, the process is really what you have to do day in and day out to be successful. We try to define the standard that we want everybody to sort of work toward, adhere to, and do it on a consistent basis. And the things that I talked about before, being responsible for your own self-determination, having a positive attitude, having great work ethic, having discipline to be able to execute on a consistent basis, whatever it is you're trying to do, those are the things that we try to focus on, and we don't try to focus as much on the outcomes as we do on being all that you can be. Eliminate the clutter and all the things that are going on outside and focus on the things that you can control with how you sort of go about and take care of your business. That's something that's ongoing, and it can never change".[4]

By focusing on the process of what the players need to do to be great, rather than on being great itself, they are able to get more out of themselves and silence their Inner Rivals.

An example of how all three goal types can work in sync:
A basketball team has the outcome goal of winning the conference title. The coach believes if they get more rebounds than their competition, they'll have a good chance of winning the game. They set the performance goal of getting more rebounds than their opponents. The coach wants the players to focus on the process goal of boxing out the other players because he believes that gives them the best chance for getting the rebound. Since the coach believes that is the best

way for their team to achieve success, they plan to focus daily practice drills around that philosophy.

Outcome goal: Win the conference title.
Performance goal: Outrebound the opponent.
Process goal: Box out opponent on every shot.

How to Set Your Goal(s)

Once you've decided on your long-term goal, the next step is to set thoughtfully your process goals. Many people find the SMART method helpful in this process. SMART goals were developed by George Doran, Arthur Miller and James Cunningham in their 1981 article "There's a S.M.A.R.T. way to write management goals and objectives". For a goal to be clear and reachable, it should be:

- Specific
- Measurable
- Actionable
- Realistic
- Time-bound

Specific

Make your process goals specific. When goals are vague, it's harder to stay committed. In one study, a group of college lacrosse players who were given more specific tasks performed substantially better than players who were simply instructed to "Do your best". By being specific with your process goals, you'll know if they're helping you reach your long-term goal. If they aren't, then you can readjust. Specific process goals would include making 50 free throws before every practice or spending 10 minutes doing meditation exercises every morning at 8 AM.

Measurable

Be sure your goals are measurable. The reason for this is similar to why they should be specific. If you can keep track and show evidence of how much you're accomplishing, then you'll know whether or not your process goal is steering you toward success. If it's not, then you know to make changes. Measuring your goal can be achieved in a variety of ways. It doesn't matter how you measure - just that you do. The above examples are measurable because you will know when you make 50 free throws or when you meditate for 10 minutes.

Actionable

You want your goal to be an action that you can claim you either did or didn't do. As a popular expression teaches, "Even the smallest deed is better than the greatest intentions." By making your goal actionable, you're setting yourself up to physically take action instead of simply intending to do so. Actionable goals would include the above examples or practicing piano 30 minutes a day, making 20 putts from 10 feet every practice, or practicing your dance routine for an hour a day.

Realistic

Setting an *unrealistic* goal is one of the biggest obstacles to success. Don't set goals that are nearly impossible to keep over a long period of time. Start with process goals you know you can achieve. Then, build up to more difficult goals.

A goal that is realistic for one person may not be realistic for someone else. It can be a realistic goal for a youth to someday play in the National Basketball Association. It is not a realistic goal for someone who is 25 and never played basketball to set the goal of playing in the NBA.

For a less extreme example, I recently set the goal of doing one hundred pull ups every other day this year. Because I have spent much of my life working out and am relatively fit, this goal is difficult, but possible. It would be unrealistic for someone to set the same goal if they were not fit or weren't able to do even one pull up. Such a person could work their way up to that same goal, but to start with that goal would be unrealistic. He or she would be less likely to stick with the goal in the long run. Instead, they could start with the process goal of going to the gym 4 days a week for an hour. As their fitness level improved, they could gradually make their process goals more difficult until reaching and surpassing the same process goal I set for myself.

Depending on how you feel at that moment and your perception of yourself, it may be difficult to come up with a realistic goal. It can be a good practice to work with someone like a coach who specializes in the area that you want to improve in order to learn more about what is realistic for you at your current level of expertise.

Time-bound
Having a start and stop time for your process goal is an important factor for knowing when you have

completed it. This doesn't necessarily need to be a literal time in minutes or hours. You just need to know when you started working on your process goal and when it's complete. An example could be making one hundred free throws. Even though it's not a "time," you know when to stop. Doing this will help you to stay disciplined on completing the goal and assisting you in gauging whether you're putting in enough time and effort to achieve your final goal.

When setting up your process goal, aim for hitting all letters of the acronym. Here are a few examples of the different elements in the SMART method working together:

- Three days a week, I go to the gym at six o'clock in the morning and make 100 free throws.
- I run ten 100-yard sprints before school for the next two weeks.
- I work on my stick handling drills after practice for 30 minutes.
- I make 30 serves before every practice this season.

By setting these goals, you hit all elements of SMART, which puts you on track for achieving your long-term goal. But it doesn't end there. To make it truly an excellent goal, turn it into a *SMART(ER)* goal! The *E* and *R* stand for *Evaluate* and *Revise.*[5]

Evaluate
As you progress with a *process goal*, evaluate it along the way to ensure it is leading you to the

long-term outcome you desire. If it seems too easy or too difficult, that's okay. You'll have the opportunity to revise and improve it. The key is to set a goal that pushes you just a bit outside your comfort zone but is not so difficult that it is completely overwhelming or causes you to quit pursuing the goal.

My goal of one hundred pull ups for 180 workouts in 2022 was originally one hundred pull ups *every day*. Before I even started, I evaluated it to see if it was realistic and achievable for me. I decided that it was better to set a goal that wasn't quite as audacious to begin with. Only if I could complete that year's goal, I would make it more difficult the next year.

Revise

If you determine that your goal is too difficult, too easy, or is not leading you to where you want to go, then take the time to revise and adjust. This will be an ongoing process as you improve in your skills and mindset, achieve more goals, and grow in the area of your choosing.

Tips for Goal Setting

Write It Down

Mark Murphy did a study called "Gender Gap and Goal-Setting. In this study he found that people who wrote down their goals were 1.2 to 1.4 times more likely to achieve their goal.[6] There is no "perfect" way to write it down. Some of the more common ways are lists, vision boards, sticky notes, and journals. Do what works for you.

Put It Somewhere You Can See It
Writing down your goal is great, but if you write it down and never look at it again, it won't do you much good. Make sure to have your goal somewhere you can see it regularly. Doing this will help to achieve your goal in two ways:

1. It keeps the goal in the forefront of your mind.
2. By seeing it often, you'll visualize yourself doing it more often (which has benefits you'll learn about in a future chapter).

From 1968-1976, Dr. Gary Hall Sr. swam on three Olympic teams for the US, earning three medals. While at Indiana University, he won eight NCAA titles and thirteen Big Ten Conference titles. He is a firm believer in writing down goals in a visible spot:

> "The two most important parts of goal setting are that you write them down and that you put them someplace where you can see them every day. I usually recommend the bathroom mirror or refrigerator door; two places I know you will always look. When I was 16-years-old, training for my first Olympic Games, my coach wrote all of my goal times down on the top of the kickboard I was using every day in practice. I couldn't escape them, but the result, after executing the plan, was that I made the Olympic team".[7]

I used this exact method when setting the goal of writing this book. In my home office, I have a desk that faces a whiteboard. In big red letters, I wrote the words "Do the work." I did this to remind myself that nothing gets done without doing the actual work. Underneath that, I wrote "Write the book" to remind myself daily of my goals so that I kept working on them even when my Inner Rival told me not to.

Have an Accountability Partner

It's extremely difficult to push yourself to achieve a long-term goal all by yourself. By having an accountability partner, you'll have someone to talk to when issues and obstacles arise. An accountability partner motivates you in times of laziness and shares in your successes, mistakes, and failures. There are many different types of accountability partners. It could be a teammate, friend, someone sharing the same goal, or a member of a shared social media group. The important thing is that they support you on your journey.

In the Dominican University study, one group was told to write down their goal and report their progress to an accountability partner. The group that did this was 76.7 percent more likely to achieve their goals than those who didn't write down their goal or have an accountability partner.[8]

Know Your WHY

Your WHY is the reason the goal is important to you. Your WHY is what pushes you to achieve your goal even when you feel like giving up. If you don't know why your goal is important to you, then it will be difficult to stay disciplined in the face of adversity. You have to know, understand, and connect with WHY your goal is important. Make sure to take the time to know your WHY!

Positive Goals

When you create your goals, keep them positive. For example, a tennis player should say, "I want to make 60 percent of my first serves." He should not say, "I don't want to miss more than 40 percent of my first serves." The first statement gives you explicit directions for what you want to do, whereas the second does not give the same level of guidance. As you will read later, whether you are telling yourself that you want to do something or that you *don't* want to do something makes a big difference.

Take the time to set goals, build a plan, and execute it. When you do the work to put this all together, not only will you have more success, but you will be better able to silence your Inner Rival.

The following exercises will help you set your goals:

Athletic Goal Dump

Brainstorm all ideas you have for things you would like to do, achieve, experience, change or develop in your world of athletics.

Come up with as many as you can. Don't judge them. Just write them down. You will decide later which goals you want to chase.

Wheel of Athletics

The wheel diagram below includes all the different factors that go into making someone a complete athlete. To be a true champion and achieve the goals you have dreamed about, you need to spend time and effort developing each of these areas.

As you fill out the wheel, think about how strong you are in each part of your development. What are your strengths and weaknesses in each specific area? Do you spend enough or any time developing that part of your game? Are there areas in which you're spending too much time developing?

Here are some sample questions for each section to get you thinking:

Skillset

Are you taking the time to learn proper technique? Are you developing strengths and weaknesses in your techniques?
Are you practicing the fundamentals consistently?

Mental Strength

Are you able to push through physically or mentally when you feel exhausted?

Do you give up easily?
How do you take instruction/criticism?

Study/ Film
Do you watch professionals in your sport and pay attention to what they do?
Do you watch film of yourself?
Do you watch film of your opponents?

Game plan/ Strategy
Do you know different types of strategies in your athletic field?
Do you know the advantages and disadvantages of those strategies?
Have you tried different strategies?

Rest/ Recovery
Are you giving your body time to recover mentally and physically?
Are you getting enough sleep?
Are you getting too much rest and sleep?

Emotional Control
Do you lose control of your emotions?
Do you enjoy the emotions you get while engaging in your sport?
Do you lose control if events don't go your way?

Nutrition
Are you drinking enough water?
Are you putting nutritious foods in your body?
Are you staying away from too many sweets and sugars?

Strength/ Fitness

Are you doing the correct types of workouts for your sport?

Are you spending enough time on the fitness side of your athletics?

Does your fitness level fit what you are trying to achieve?

Interpreting Your Wheel

Be as honest as possible about where you are in your development. Even the top performers in your sport won't score a ten in every category on the wheel. There will always be room for improvement.

If this were a real wheel, how bumpy would the ride be? You are aiming to have all segments scored evenly (or close), above seven, and as near ten as possible.

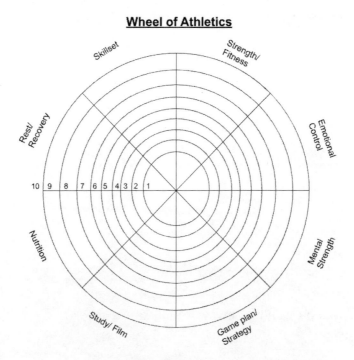

Wheel of Athletics

Goal Breakdown and Development

- List your goal(s).
- Assign your goals into their respective categories (outcome, performance, process. Create smaller goals that will help you achieve your long-term goal.
- Write down SMARTER goals that can help you reach you short-term goals.

Long-Term Goal	Short-Term Goals	SMARTER Goals

Chapter 2

MINDFUL MEDITATION & FOCUSED BREATHING

"... Lebron James sitting courtside during the 2013 NBA playoffs, only instead of concentrating on something outside of himself, James had his eyes closed and was focusing within, even with the same commotion around him. James was no doubt concentrating on his breathing, clearing space in his mind so that he could get into conscious flow and sustain it when he returned to the game"[9]

The Inner Rival

Your Inner Rival, if left unchecked, can produce constant chatter in your mind that can create and enhance the emotional ups and downs inside of you. It takes your focus away from what you can control and steers it toward things you are powerless to change. It makes you dwell on all the mistakes you may have made in the past or on regrets about how you wish you would have acted differently. It also can push your thoughts to the future, making you anxious about how different situations will turn out or worry about things you have no control over.

By becoming more mindful, you will begin to silence the constant noise in your head and enjoy just being in the moment and experiencing it fully.

You will learn to use meditation and breath control to teach you how to be in the moment. It will be an exercise to develop your ability to respond thoughtfully to life's events. You'll learn to be less affected mentally and emotionally by the craziness of life around you and better equipped to respond positively during competition and in your daily life.

Introduction

What do Michael Jordan, Derek Jeter, Kobe Bryant, and Carli Lloyd have in common? They're all world-class athletes, but they share more than that. Each one has reported using the practice of meditation at one point or another to become more mindful and help reach their peak athletic performance. There's a reason so many top performers throughout the world in sports, business, and entertainment use meditation in their daily lives and their training and preparation. It works!

Tim Ferris, who has written best-selling books such as *The 4-Hour Work Week* and *Tribe of Mentors*, interviewed 140 top performers in their respective fields. He found roughly 80 percent of them did mindful meditation in their daily routine.[10] But for many athletes and society in general, practicing mindfulness and meditation is not even a blip on their radar. This omission is most likely because it is difficult to see the results of mindfulness practice. But the results are most definitely felt by those who practice it daily.

Meditation has gained more popularity over the last few decades. This reality is not surprising with its reported ability to help reduce feelings of depression, anxiety, and stress.[11] I know from personal experience that since I have incorporated meditation of various forms into my life, my stress and anxiety levels have decreased significantly. I have become more mindful of how I respond to adverse situations. I am less likely to react negatively, as well as, much quicker to realize when my mind has wandered and the chatter has taken over. There is no doubt that meditation has had a positive impact on my life.

The development of this practice can substantially impact your mindset and emotional control when you're in the heat of competition or living your daily life. Our society has often viewed meditation as hokey, or a technique used by monks on top of a mountain. But in actuality it's a worldly and wise practice that can change your life the way that it has for countless others throughout history. Don't take the word "meditation" as something that needs to be complicated. You don't have to get into some crazy pose like you're in Cirque du Soleil and sit for hours (although you can if you really want to). It really can be as simple as sitting and focusing on your breathing for a few minutes. But just because something is simple doesn't mean it's easy.

In this chapter I will lay out the idea of mindfulness and its importance. I'll speak about some benefits you can experience as a person and athlete if you build meditation into your daily routine. I'll also explain how you can start to practice meditation and mindfulness for yourself.

Mindfulness

Mindfulness simply means being in the moment, right here, right now, detached from your thoughts. Dr. Jon Kabat-Zinn, a mindfulness leader, describes mindfulness as "the awareness that arises from paying attention, on purpose, in the present moment and non-judgmentally" to yourself and the environment around you.[12] It includes the ability not to let all the chatter in your mind take you away from the moment at hand. It's calming down your racing thoughts and just *being*.

For so many of us, our minds are constantly wandering. Often, they are in the past ruminating over something we wish we did or didn't do. If not, they're in the future worrying about conversations you need to have with a coworker, a big meeting next week, or an upcoming game. That's the exact opposite of mindfulness. With mindful meditation and focused breathing, you can learn to bring your mind back to the current moment.

Dr. Kabat-Zinn trained the 1984 Olympic men's rowing team in mindfulness. He described mindfulness meditation as using "different objects [on which] to focus one's attention, and it could be a focus on sensations of breathing, or emotions, or thoughts, or observing any type of body sensations...But it's about bringing the mind back to the here and now, as opposed to letting the mind drift".[13] Focusing on your breath or a sensation in your body anchors your mind and emotions into the moment so they don't roam wildly. This intentionality happens right at that moment when you focus on a feeling or your breathing. You have, at that moment, stopped your mind from a constant stream of chatter. With the average person having roughly 6,200 thoughts a day, learning to calm those thoughts and direct them mindfully is an essential part of developing mental strength.[14] Granted, you'll not always be 100 percent focused on the moment, but the more you can be here and now, the better off you'll be.

Let's simplify it even more. The overall idea of mindfulness can be summed up with one sentence, "Be where your feet are." Whether playing your sport, working on a paper, or hanging out with friends, be in the moment where your feet are. Though the concept seems simple, it's not easy.

Practicing mindfulness has become a big part of my daily life in recent years. Throughout my day, when I catch my mind wandering, I do my best to bring it back into the moment. I often do this by focusing on a few deep, slow breaths and then refocusing my attention or concentrating on one of my senses and taking in what is happening. If I am somewhere with lovely scenery, I will try to focus more on what I see. If I'm working out, I will try to direct my attention to the muscles working during that exercise. If I am outside or listening to music, I will focus more on what I hear. By doing this, I can bring my mind back to the moment. This response happens countless times throughout the day, as our minds all tend to wander. When I'm going for a walk, cleaning the house, driving, working out, or in the company of friends and family, I try to be in the moment. There are days when this is easier, and then there are days when I feel like my mind is racing and can't slow down. Those days where I struggle to focus are the most vital for me to take some time to slow down and figure out why my mind is filled with chatter.

I believe wholeheartedly that this practice has helped develop and strengthen my ability to appreciate much more of what life offers. We miss so much of what happens around us because we are too caught up in our own heads. Taking the time to practice mindfulness is not an easy practice to work on, but one that will most definitely enhance your life.

Mindfulness and "The Zone"

Most athletes know about the flow state, otherwise known as being in "the zone." It's a state of supreme focus, so completely immersed in an activity that time seems to disappear. When you're in the "the zone," your actions become less thought out and more automatic. When this happens, athletes often have their optimal performances. We've all been there many times, whether we realize it or not. So how does mindfulness help to make this happen?

This flow state comes from an athlete's ability to disengage from distractions and entirely focus on the here and now.[15] Meditation has the ability to create an easier path into "the zone." In 2011, a study was done to investigate the effects of a CD-based mindfulness program on elite athletes and their ability to get into the flow state over a six-week period. Thirteen university athletes were split up randomly into two groups, one receiving the CD-based mindfulness training and the other receiving no mindfulness training. Results showed the athletes who went through the training program experienced a greater sense of flow than those in the control group who did not receive any mindfulness training.[16] The higher level an athlete reaches, the more important the ability to get into flow state or "the zone" becomes.

Meditation

Meditation is a practice and a means to mindfulness. Meditation is a way to build your awareness of your thoughts and actions. It's a tried-and-true method used for centuries by many spiritual and philosophical traditions such as Buddhism, Christianity, Stoicism, Taoism, yoga, and Tai Chi. It's not religious in and of itself. It's an exercise you can do for as little as one minute a day and still feel the benefits after a few weeks. Like any other skill, the more you practice, the more you'll reap the benefits.

The world is full of chaos, much of which you cannot control, and it doesn't seem to be slowing down anytime soon. The more it happens in and around you, the more difficult it becomes to be in the moment. By using meditation to improve and strengthen your mindfulness and ability to focus when you're in the calm of life, you will increase your awareness and ability to stay mindful amid adversity and stressful situations. Much of the worry and doubt you experience in life stems from fixing your attention on things outside your control or getting caught up in your racing thoughts. By building meditation into your daily routine, you'll become more aware of when your mind is wandering or focusing on something you can't control. You then can bring your mind back to the moment.

Why is this important? Imagine yourself with two minutes left in the game and the score tied, meeting with a potential massive sale for your company, or fighting with a close friend or family member. All these situations are emotionally charged. We can quickly be taken away by our thoughts and feelings. When that happens, bad decisions result. Being mindful in those situations will allow you to make better choices on how you respond.

Buddhist priest and author Bodhin Kjolhede presented an excellent visual of how meditation works in his TEDx presentation. He compares the mind to a snow globe and each snowflake as a thought. The snow spinning around a shaken snow globe is like your mind racing with ideas that you can't seem to settle down. Meditation allows you to set the snow globe down and let your mind rest as the snowflakes fall gently to the ground. It helps to relieve the chaos that can swirl around in our minds.[17] As you practice meditation when life is calm, you become better able to transfer those skills and benefits during the more chaotic situations in your life.

Lifeboat Versus Submarine

Picture a small lifeboat sitting on the ocean's surface. The water is calm and glistening in the early morning, allowing you to paddle freely. It is easy to control your boat, just like your mind and thoughts are when there's no stress in your life. Now imagine that little boat when thunder and high winds come roaring along. The boat gets tossed around, and you cannot control where it goes. This chaos is what your thoughts and emotions feel like when life gets stressful and you're unable to be mindful. The outside world dictates what happens to you emotionally and mentally and, in turn, creates fear, anxiety, and negative stress.

By regularly practicing meditation, you'll feel more like a submarine that can go well below the surface rather than a small boat that can quickly capsize. You can observe the storm raging on the surface and all the things outside of you that you can't control. Though you may still be slightly affected by what's going on around you, staying mindful will be much easier. Meditation and focused breathing can give you the capability to observe and view what's happening around and within you without allowing your thoughts and emotions to capsize in the storm and chaos of life.

Imagine yourself stepping up to the free-throw line in the game's final seconds. Winning or losing the state title depends on whether you make these shots. If you haven't practiced meditation, you will begin to feel like the lifeboat and get tossed around by all these different factors. Your body's fundamental physiological response will take over. Your mind starts to race and fill up with potential adverse outcomes. Your focus gets pulled away by all the noises and tension around you. You become preoccupied with what your friends, family, teammates, and coaches will think if you miss this shot. You worry about disappointing your team and fans. You obsess over the fact that everyone is counting on you. Your breaths shorten, your heart begins to beat wildly, and your muscles tighten up. You overthink specific movements you performed automatically in the past, which causes a lower chance of success.[18] When this happens, all you can do is your best to force a good result.

If you have practiced daily meditation, you will feel more like a submarine in these difficult situations. You will notice some negative thoughts and distractions, but you will have the ability to disengage your mind from those distractions and focus more on what you can control. By clearing mentally from those distractions, you are less likely to be overcome by the emotions in the situation. You will have a better chance of producing the outcome that you hope for.

Reaction Versus Response

"Between stimulus and response, there is a space. In that space is our power to choose our response. In our response lies our growth and our freedom. "This quote has been used for years. The original author is unknown. Although we don't know to whom the credit belongs, the power and wisdom behind the quote have never been questioned.

In our world, negative stimuli are everywhere. It can be a car swerving in front of you on the highway, a rude comment made by someone in line at the post office, or a bad call made by a referee at a ball game. When you *react* to a stimulus, it's quick, emotional, usually not thought out, and often something you will regret. Reaction frequently shows itself in anger, frustration, guilt, pity, anxiety, or fear. It is a type of defense mechanism for the mind. Often when we *react* to something, we'll regret that reaction in the long run because it stems from an emotional flareup rather than sound decision-making.

By contrast, a *response* is more reflective and less emotionally charged. It comes from a place of calm and strength rather than a place of chaos, anxiety, and fear. It's a choice of how to act in a situation based on your core values, not an action dictated by a quick emotional reaction.

By meditating, you begin to develop your attentional control you choose what you pay attention to and what to ignore. You start to mentally lengthen the feeling of time between stimulus and response. That feeling of added time frees your mind. It empowers you to choose thoughtfully your answer rather than *reacting* uncontrollably and emotionally to the stimulus.

As a tennis player, overreacting is something with which I struggled mightily. Meditation helps slow down my thinking and lessen my overt reactions to stimuli. Rather than reacting, I'm better equipped to recognize the feelings as they come up inside me and choose my response. By no means have I perfected this, but there's no doubt that meditation has helped silence my Inner Rival.

Hall of Fame and three-time Super Bowl-winning quarterback Troy Aikman has been practicing meditation for about ten years. In a 2022 article, he reflected on how meditation and mindfulness would have changed his play during his years with the Dallas Cowboys. "Now, part of my practice is not being reactionary, and I think I was highly reactionary when I played. So, I think from that standpoint, I wouldn't have reacted the same way. I wouldn't have reacted nearly as often to whatever the circumstance was".[19] Aikman learned years after playing the difference between reacting and responding in football and life.

Physical Effects of Meditation on the Brain

Meditation not only offers attentional and emotional benefits but physical benefits as well. The more you meditate, the more your brain develops. It's not instant, but by practicing a few minutes each day, you'll feel the changes in your mindset within a couple of weeks.[20]

One of the physical benefits you will experience occurs in your prefrontal cortex.[21] The prefrontal cortex is your brain's control panel, providing concentration, awareness, impulse control, and emotional reactions. It makes up roughly 40 percent of your brain. Meditation, when done routinely, has been shown to strengthen substantially and thicken this area of the brain. All of those functions thus become stronger and more prevalent in your life. Sounds great, doesn't it? It gets better!

Another vital area of the brain that benefits from meditation is the amygdala, associated with emotions, fight or flight, and stress.[22] About the size of two almonds, the amygdala is located near the center of your brain and is part of the limbic system. Studies have shown that by meditating daily, the brain's cell volume in the amygdala decreases over time, which has been linked to lower stress levels.[23]

Meditation will also strengthen the link *between* the prefrontal cortex and amygdala, which link tends to give the prefrontal cortex greater control of our emotions, stress, and anxiety. With this control comes more feelings of calm, patience, and resilience. These feelings are extremely important when facing an intense situation, especially in athletics, where the emotional ups and downs can happen very quickly.

Meditation and Focus

You'll miss opportunities to achieve incredible feats if you allow yourself to become distracted or side-tracked too often. Success in any field requires focus. And the key to improving your focus is meditation. Meditating strengthens your focus and attention span, just as weightlifting strengthens your muscles. You become better able to focus more intently for extended periods. One study took random subjects between 18-45 years of age who had not practiced meditation before. The study put them through a 13-minute daily meditation routine for eight weeks. Compared to the control group (who listened to a podcast for 13-minutes daily instead of meditating), the meditators experienced a decrease in negative mood, enhanced attention and working memory, and decreased state anxiety.[24] These results are all crucial to achieving your goal, no matter what it is or how difficult it may seem.

Picture yourself in a dark room holding a flash-light. The flashlight you're holding is your focus. If you haven't meditated, you don't have great control of your focus, and your flashlight will shine on what-ever movement or sound catches your attention. The light of your flashlight will bounce from one commo-tion to another and never really focus on anything.

This illustration could be the difference between a win and a loss in a competition.

The attention of someone who has practiced meditation regularly remains more stable and focused. They can shine the flashlight where *they* choose rather than the light starting to flicker and wander away at the first distraction they notice. No matter what other disturbances occur, those who regularly practice meditation can better keep the focus directed where they know it will be most beneficial.

Imagine you're competing for the state championship. Thousands of fans are cheering in the stands, music is playing, teammates and coaches are yelling, and opponents are in your face trying to stop you from doing what you want. Do you know who else is there trying to stop you? Your Inner Rival, and it's been waiting for the right moment to strike. To perform at your peak in a moment like this, you must have the skills to place your focus where it's helpful. If your mind wanders and outside sources take over your thoughts, you'll have difficulty succeeding.

Meditation also helps your focus by decreasing attentional blink.[25] Attentional blink is when multiple objects or stimuli are presented to you. Your brain can get stuck on the first object and cannot react to the second one. A hockey goalie needs to pay attention both to where the opponent is and where the puck is going on the shot. Regular meditation reduces the tendency to get stuck on distracting stimuli or thoughts of self-doubt and worry. You will still be aware of the distractions, but you'll have the strength to break free from them at that moment.

Focused Breathing

In his book, *Unbeatable Mind,* Navy SEAL Commander Mark Divine states, "To say that learning breath control is the most important component to forging mental toughness would not be an overstatement".[26] Developing the ability to focus on your breathing is one of the simplest and most effective approaches when working on meditation and mindfulness. Your breath can be used as an "anchor" that can continually bring you back into the moment when your mind begins to wander. While meditating, you calm the mind and concentrate on one thing. Inevitably your mind will start to stray. When you notice that happening, use your "anchor" or breathing to bring you back into the moment.

The way you breathe in life has a massive impact on your stress and anxiety levels. If you feel stressed and anxious, your breathing will generally become short, jerky, shallow, and from your upper chest. This often is followed by a high level of negative energy, emotions, and thoughts. By controlling your breathing pattern with slower, longer breaths from your diaphragm, you'll have better control of your levels of stress.

Breathing and Emotions

Not only do your emotions affect your breathing, but your breathing can also influence your emotions. Changing your breathing style and pattern can alter your emotional state. Catherine Dowling is the author of multiple books on breathing and a clinical practitioner of breathwork psychotherapy in Ireland for over twenty years. She cites a study on the relationship between breathing and emotions entitled, "Respiratory Feedback in the Generation of Emotion"[27].

This study included two groups of volunteers. The first group was asked to produce four emotions: sadness, fear, anger, and joy using memory, fantasy, and breathing modification. Scientists then monitored and analyzed the breathing patterns for the various emotions. They studied the speed, location in the lungs, and amplitude of the breathing and then used their findings to write instructions for breathing.

These written instructions were then given to the volunteers in group two. The volunteers were asked to breathe according to those written instructions from the earlier experiment. After a 45-minute breathing session, they were asked to fill out a questionnaire designed to elicit a range of information, including detail of their emotional response. The results showed that the four breathing patterns created the anticipated emotional reactions to varying but significant degrees.

They discovered that breathing slowly and deeply into the belly can help reduce the grip of anxiety, fear, and anger. When you find your emotions taking over, you can reduce stress at that moment by slow, deep belly breathing. Whenever I feel overwhelmed, a few long, deep breaths from my diaphragm will give me the time to slow my mind and think more rationally. It allows me to choose the responses I want to make rather than react immediately.

The Philippot study demonstrates how important it is to be aware of your breathing in a stressful situation.[28] When facing nervousness or anxiety, breathing often becomes short and choppy and stems from your upper chest. With practice, you can learn to redirect your breathing to be longer and slower and originate more deeply in your diaphragm. This can make a massive difference in the success you see in your sport, work-life relationships and health. Make sure you take the time to focus and learn to control your breathing.

Meditation Exercise: Getting Started

If you're serious about adding mindful meditation and focused breathing to your daily routine, there are many resources available, including apps for your phone. For now, here are a couple of short exercises to give you an idea of how to meditate mindfully:

Exercise 1

Begin by finding a quiet place to sit down. It can be on the floor or in a chair. Give yourself a few seconds to get comfortable and gently close your eyes.

1. Take a few deep breaths starting from your belly region.
2. Breath in through your nose, filling your lungs to the count of four.
3. Hold for four seconds.
4. Exhale through your mouth for four seconds.
5. Hold your breath for four seconds.
6. Repeat.
7. After a couple of repetitions, do your best to let go of your thoughts. Focus on your breathing. In...and out. In...and out.

Please don't get frustrated when you notice your mind is starting to wander away from focusing on your breathing (and it will). Kindly and gently bring it back to the present moment and refocus on your breathing again. If you begin by trying to sit for a long time, the likelihood you'll quit increases substantially. Introduce the exercise into your routine by starting with one minute a day. It's challenging to sit in stillness for that length of time, let alone for five, ten, or thirty-minute sessions. As it becomes a habit and feels easier, slowly increase the length of time you spend practicing.

Exercise 2

1. Find a comfortable place to sit outside and close your eyes.
2. Take a minute to notice the different scents wafting around you.
3. Then focus on the various sounds around you. Nearby sounds and far-off sounds.
4. Feel your arms and legs resting. Feel your feet on the ground. Notice the air. Is it windy? Is it hot or cold out?

By spending time noticing the different sensations in your body, you're living in that moment. The more you practice doing exercises like this, the easier it'll be to stay in the moment when you genuinely want or need to be.

There are many different ways to work on mindfulness and meditation. The above exercises are a great place to start. But the key is to find a method that works best for you and do it consistently.

Chapter 3

VISUALIZATION

As legend has it, Major James Nesmith was a pilot for the US during the Vietnam war. While on a mission, he was shot down and captured as a prisoner of war. He was kept in a cage for years in an area filled with bugs and other undesirable things. Desperate to find a way to pass time, he began to visualize himself playing golf at his favorite course back home for hours a day. He would picture every little detail that he could. His grip, stance, swing, flight of the ball, trees, grass, and much more. He made sure that every shot he hit was perfect. If it wasn't, he would do it again. Then he would picture himself walking to the ball and preparing for the next shot. After his release from the camp, he went back home and played his favorite course again. He shot twenty strokes better than he ever had before.[29]

The Inner Rival

Your Inner Rival will use negative images to show you the worst that can happen in attempts to keep you from taking a risk, moving out of your comfort zone, and trying to grow. Whether you're getting ready for an important game, a big speech, dance performance, or a difficult conversation with a friend, your Inner Rival will try to magnify all the potential negative outcomes to keep you in your comfort zone. It's vital to combat it by visualizing success.

By learning to use visualization that is positive and constructive, your mind will be filled with images of you succeeding and overcoming the obstacles and challenges ahead. You'll see yourself being victorious despite the difficult circumstances around you. In this chapter I will explain what the practice of visualization is, why it will benefit you to add it to your routine, and how you can include it in your training.

What is Visualization?

Visualization is a practice that can benefit anyone when it's used regularly. This is especially true for athletics and performance activities. Visualization can be defined as "an experience that mimics real experience. We can be aware of 'seeing' an image, feeling movements as an image, or experiencing an image of smell, tastes, or sounds without actually experiencing the real thing".[30] A simplified explanation would be using your "mind's eye" to imagine yourself in various situations. The goal is to picture yourself successfully completing a task. This may sound easy to do, but it can be much more difficult than you might think.

Visualization is a technique that has been used for decades by professional athletes, comedians, special forces operators, musicians, speakers, actors, and teachers. Taking the time to picture yourself overcoming obstacles and succeeding can have a massive impact on your outcome. Just like any other skill, if you don't practice it on a regular basis, you won't receive much benefit from it. But if you build it into your daily routine, it will become a strong and positive tool in your mental toolbox.

Many top-level performers use visualization because the brain is unable to tell the difference between a real activity and one that's imagined. When an athlete pictures themselves doing a movement or taking a shot, the same circuits are activated in the brain as if they're actually experiencing it. If a softball player imagines hitting a curveball for a home run, their brain believes they hit a curveball for a home run. Scientists in the sports field often refer to this as "Functional Equivalence." Sport Psychologist Richard Suinn hooked up downhill skiers to an EMG machine, which is used to detect muscle movements. When the skiers only imagined themselves downhill skiing, they activated the exact same muscles they would have used while actually downhill skiing, even though they weren't moving.[31]

Other studies have shown the use of visualization may play a positive role on a person's immunity, stress, pain management, and self-esteem.[32] With so many positives that come from the use of this tool, there's no doubt that learning to use it correctly will have a substantial impact on your growth and success.

There are different ways to visualize, but I believe the most beneficial technique for performance and athletics is *polysensory imagery*. This is the ability to use all your senses (sound, sight, smell, touch, taste), emotions and body movements to imagine yourself in the situation. Neuroscience has proven that the brain is capable of reproducing mental images from all the senses, including pressures, temperatures, and textures. For the duration of this book, the word *visualization* refers to poly-sensory imagery.

Benefits of Visualization

Whether you're a boxer, teacher, CEO, tennis player, or hockey coach, you will find value in using visualization to enhance your performance.

Increased Strength
There's no substitute for physical work and lifting weights when it comes to getting stronger and more fit, but studies are beginning to show that visualization can help to increase muscle strength. Researchers at Ohio University wrapped the wrists of 29 volunteers, so they were immobilized for a month. Half of the group visualized themselves flexing their muscles for eleven minutes a day, five days a week while the other group did nothing. The study found that when the casts were removed, the group members who visualized flexing their wrists were two times stronger than those who did not.[33] If you find yourself physically unable to do the workout, whether from injury or lack of equipment, taking time to do it mentally would offer more benefit than doing nothing at all.

Improved Reaction Time

In most sports, reaction time can make the difference between makes and misses, wins and losses, champions and all the rest. Athletes, coaches, and trainers are always looking for ways to be quicker. Visualization can help you do that. In a 2016 study of 200 mixed martial arts fighters, researchers found that regular visualization and self-talk practice reduced fighters' reaction time from 0.737 to 0.659 seconds.[34] That is nearly 10 percent, which may not sound like much but can make a huge difference when trying to hit a 90-mph fastball, 130-mph serve in tennis, or dodging a punch!

Improved Skill

Since we know the same areas of the brain light up whether we are actually doing an activity or imagining it, visualization is a wonderful tool for improving a skill. While at the University of Chicago, Dr. Judd Biasiotto conducted an experiment using visualization to improve the skill of free throw shooting. He pulled together a group of random students, had them shoot free throws, and tallied how many each student made. He then broke them up into three groups with different requirements for practice.[35]

- Group 1 was told not to touch a basketball for thirty days.
- Group 2 had to go to the gym every day and shoot free throws for thirty minutes.
- Group 3 had to go to the gym every day, close their eyes, and visualize themselves making free throws for thirty minutes.

They came back together after the thirty days and shot free throws again.

- Group 1: Did not show any improvement
- Group 2: Improved by 24 percent
- Group 3: Improved by 23 percent

This shows us that using visualization is an effective tool for improving a skill. But if you use only visualization over a long period of time without doing the actual physical work, you won't see the same level of improvement. Because both are helpful at improving skill, it is recommended you use both methods to sharpen your skills for peak performance.

It would have been interesting to see the changes had there been a fourth group who both practiced physically as well as used visualization. Instead, I will leave that up to you to see how effective it is!

Improved Focus

The ability to focus on what's most important at any given moment is essential to your success. In many situations, especially in athletics, there is plenty of stimulus to take your attention away from the main objective. Imagine you're either a basketball player competing in a crowded gym, a football player about to kick a field goal to win the game in a visitor's stadium, or a substitute teacher standing in front of a room of thirty rowdy students. The amount of stimulus in each situation can be overwhelming if you don't know how to direct your attention. Visualization can help that.

Visualization activates your Reticular Activating System (RAS), which is a network of neurons located in the brain stem. It helps to filter out the unnecessary information so you can focus on what's important to you.[36] It has been said your brain perceives up to two billion pieces of data per second through the five senses, but it can only process roughly 126 pieces.[37] That process is done by the RAS. By using visualization to picture yourself in situations that require focus, your RAS will better understand what's important and what's not in advance of those real-life situations.

A good example of this occurs when a basketball player is shooting a free throw and the crowd behind the basket goes crazy to distract them. For someone who doesn't play basketball, it can seem extremely distracting. But for someone who works on this skill, the crowd behind the basket doesn't seem nearly as distracting (most of the time) because the player's RAS has been trained to focus on the rim.

Boosted Confidence

Your confidence level plays a large factor in just about every area of life. The tricky thing about confidence is it can be there one minute and gone the next. It is even more challenging to recover it once it's gone. Visualization is a great tool to build confidence, maintain it, and even detect when it has slipped away.

Connor McGregor is a top-level mixed martial arts fighter. His trainer, John Kavanagh, describes how McGregor uses visualization to boost his confidence. He talks about how McGregor had gone through the fight thousands of times in his head even before he gets to the arena. He visualizes what it will be like backstage warming up pre-fight, what the crowd would sound and look like, and how the arena would smell. He would do these weeks in advance leading up to the fight, so that he wouldn't be surprised when walking out for the fight for the first time.[38]

Visualization is such an effective tool because so much of self-confidence comes from previous success and familiarity. As Kavanagh mentioned, if you were to walk into an arena of fifteen thousand people yelling while you were preparing to go fight for the first time, it could feel quite overwhelming. But if you previously had visualized the various sensations you may encounter, you will most likely feel more prepared and less uncomfortable. You'll have been there before in your mind.

Let's use an example that many of us can relate to: the first day at a new school. On your way there, you probably experienced some level of apprehension about the new environment, teachers, students, and class schedule. As the year went on, the nervousness most likely lessened while your confidence increased. You came to know what to expect. The more you visualize yourself in situations you may encounter, the more comfortable you'll feel. This is what visualization can do for you.

Styles of Visualization

By using the right type of visualization for your situation, you'll get even more out of it. There are four general types of visualization: Specific Motivation, General Motivation, Specific Cognitive, General Cognitive.[39] Each of them is beneficial when used in the appropriate circumstances.

Specific Motivation

This style of visualization requires you to picture specific outcomes or achievements. This type is good to use when you want to achieve an outcome goal or a desired result. If you want to make a team, you might visualize your name on the list, imagine hearing the coach say, "you made the team," or picture yourself playing the sport in the team jersey. Maybe you want to win a championship, so you picture yourself hitting the game-winning shot or making the game-winning save in a shootout. It should be something that motivates and positions you to be successful in your event.

I personally use this type of visualization often. In writing this book and building a profession working with teams and businesses, I have pictured myself in several different types of situations and settings in which I'm working to help others silence their Inner Rival. Even though I may be entering an unfamiliar environment, I feel more comfortable and confident when I get there because I have visualized already being there.

General Motivation

In this version of visualization, you see yourself being successful in whatever you are doing to help keep you motivated. It is often used in conjunction with positive self-talk. General Motivation helps you stay motivated and positive while pursuing your goal or peak performance. This version is great for controlling emotions, mindset, and breathing while in situations that are stressful or cause high levels of arousal. A 2010 study was done using fifty elite tennis players with similar physical abilities, 25 of them as the experimental group and 25 as the control. The group who used mental imagery during the sport had a significant reduction to their scores on an anxiety questionnaire compared to the group who didn't use mental imagery.[40] When preparing for a big game, speech, or an unfamiliar situation, this type of visualization will help you maintain control and positivity.

Specific Cognitive

Use this type of visualization when you want to picture yourself performing a certain skill perfectly. It is often what people think of when they hear the word visualization. You imagine yourself performing a skill such as throwing a pitch over the strike zone, kicking a field goal through the uprights, or chipping the ball onto the green. Picture the movements and imagine all the sensations that go along with performing the task. Be sure your visual exercise ends with a positive outcome. That may sound obvious, but you would be surprised at how difficult doing so can be.

Specific cognitive visualization is powerful. I've personally experienced its effects both positively and negatively. I've enjoyed playing golf for several years and am a halfway decent player. When I step up to address the ball, if a negative image enters my mind before I swing, I almost always hit the ball the way I imagined—very poorly. I have learned that when the negative image appears while I am addressing the ball, I need to take a deep breath while briefly imagining a good shot before I swing. Now, this doesn't always produce a perfect shot, but the number of bad shots has dropped dramatically. PGA Tour here I come!

I'm not the only "amazing" golfer preaching the importance of using visualization. Professional golfer and winner of eighteen PGA majors, Jack Nicklaus mentioned it in multiple interviews. He says, "I never hit a shot, not even in practice, without having a very sharp, in-focus picture of it in my head. First, I see the ball where I want it to finish, nice and white and sitting up high on the bright green grass. Then, the scene quickly changes, and I see the ball going there: its path, trajectory, and shape, even its behavior on landing. Then, there is a sort of fade-out, and the next scene shows me making the kind of swing that will turn the previous images into reality".[41] To reach Nicklaus' level of visualization skill takes time and practice but if you work on it, you will have a huge advantage over the competition.

General Cognitive

Here you are visualizing yourself being successful in different situations. I personally believe this type of visualization doesn't get used enough. With so much emphasis on visualizing success, people often forget about picturing themselves overcoming difficult situations or setbacks. Imagine yourself on the basketball court with your team down ten points with five minutes left on the clock. Or picture yourself turned over on your back in a wrestling match having to fight your way out of it. When you do this, you're placing yourself in a situation where you must make a comeback from a challenge. People often only visualize themselves being successful, which is great, but when they encounter a setback, they're unprepared. If you can visualize yourself being successful as well as overcoming setbacks, you'll be ready for whatever the competition throws at you.

Perspective

There are two different perspectives you can have while visualizing. One is first person or internal, in which you're viewing from your own eyes. The other is third person or external, in which you're picturing yourself doing the activity from an observer's perspective. Third person is similar to watching yourself at the movies. Neither one is necessarily better than another. Both are good for different situations. You also can be like Jack Nicklaus and use both to your advantage.

First Person Perspective

First person works well when you're picturing yourself making a shot or performing a skill with a successful outcome. Viewing it from your perspective can help create a more realistic feel. You can break down the movements of the action and make sure they're done correctly. Your muscles will fire up your brain as if you're experiencing the action in real time. But if you're new to a particular activity and don't have a lot of physical experience in the skill, first person may not be as helpful. You're not as familiar with the body movements and how they feel when performed successfully.

First person is good for preparing to respond to different situations. Examples include returning a serve in tennis, hitting a fastball, or defending a barrage of punches in mixed martial arts. All these activities force you to respond to stimuli in a very short amount of time. By picturing a first-person point of view and responding to these stimuli successfully, you'll increase your chance of success in real life.

Third Person Perspective

Third person is a great way to build your motivation and see yourself overcome difficult situations. Whether it's your team making a comeback, or you are doing spins and flips in gymnastics or hoisting the championship trophy, picturing these situations can actually increase your chances of success. Your brain doesn't know the difference between real and imagined. Every time you visualize yourself being successful, your brain believes it.

I often use third person perspective visualization before speaking in front of a group. I see myself on stage or in front of the group as if I were an audience member. I see myself standing, moving around, and speaking comfortably. I find the more I do this, the less nervous I am. Even if I make a mistake or something happens that I can't control, I'm able to roll with it and not let it affect my performance.

Two Tips for Effective Visualization

1. Keep It Positive.

Make sure when you're visualizing your activity, you construct the ending with a positive or successful outcome. It won't necessarily happen inherently. You may visualize yourself missing the shot or putt, which is completely normal since our mind tends to naturally go toward the negative. If that happens, visualize the action again with a positive outcome.

2. *Make It Detailed.*

When visualizing your performance or skill, make sure it's as detailed and vivid as possible. The more realistic it is, the more you'll benefit from the practice. If you imagine yourself teeing off in a golf tournament, imagine all the details. View the ball from your perspective. Feel the texture of the glove, the weight of the club in your hands, and the temperature of the wind blowing in your face. Notice the people around you. Imagine the sensations in your body when you take the club back while your eyes are still on the ball. Add the sensation of contact and follow through while watching the flight of the ball going where you want it to. It takes time and practice to imagine something this detailed but it's about quality over quantity. It'll get easier with time.

The following exercises will help you learn to use visualization:

Exercise 1

1. Close your eyes and take three deep slow breaths.
2. Picture an apple.
   - What color is it?
   - Is it shiny or dull?
   - Is it big or small?
   - Are there any bruises on it?
   - Is there a stem?
   - Is it sitting on anything?
3. Now pick up the apple.
   - Is it heavy?
   - Is it smooth or rough?
   - Hard or mushy?
4. Take a bite of the apple.
   - Is it crunchy?
   - Warm or cold?
   - Is it sweet or tart?
   - Is it juicy?

Exercise 2

Go into a dark room with a lit candle. Set the candle on the table or desk and sit down next to it. Stare at the flame for ten to fifteen seconds, and then close your eyes. Chances are, you can still see the flame for a few seconds once you close your eyes. Work on trying to extend the time you're imagining the flame once you close your eyes.

Exercise 3

Close your eyes and picture a room with which you're very familiar. Maybe it's your kitchen or bedroom. Imagine all the little details on the walls, tables, desks, etc. Then think about any sounds or smells associated with that room. As you get better at this, begin to change colors or objects around the room in your mental image.

Chapter 4

CONTROL THE CONTROLLABLE

"You have power over your mind—not outside events. Realize this, and you will find strength."
—Marcus Aurelius

The Inner Rival

Your Inner Rival will trick you into believing that you have control over more than you actually do. It will tell you, "Life isn't fair," and "you need to worry about what other people say or do." It creates stress, worry, doubt, and fear going into situations out of your control. Learning to focus on what you *can* control will begin to eliminate that stress, worry, doubt and fear. In this chapter, I'll share the tools to focus on what you can control and to forget about the rest.

Understanding Control

Michael Phelps is the most decorated Olympian of all time with twenty-eight medals, of which twenty-three are gold. Achieving such an amazing feat required training for all types of situations. Phelps' coach, Bob Bowman, wanted Michael to learn to focus on what *he* could control no matter the circumstances. To prepare him for the unexpected, Bowman would do things like change Michael's training times at the last minute and ban him from drinking water on breaks. Bowman's teachings even included breaking Phelps goggles right before a race to see how he'd react when they filled up with water. This action actually proved to be extremely helpful in 2008 at the Beijing Olympics. When Phelps was in the final heat of the 200m butterfly, his goggles began to fill up with water. Because he was trained to focus on what he could control, Phelps didn't panic. He went on to win that race essentially blind.[42]

Having the power to focus only on what you can control is much more difficult than it sounds. A high percentage of what we stress and worry about are outside of our control. We cannot control the traffic on the way to work or an appointment, what a coworker said about us the other day, the coach putting someone else in the starting line-up, or what someone thinks of you! We have absolutely NO control over those things. Why then, do we worry and stress about them so much?

We worry because we want to be in control. The more we try to control everything, especially what we can't control, the more anxious we feel. Then we try to control more of our lives and get even more anxious! It's a vicious cycle that can result in bad habits of blaming others, holding on to anger, or relieving stress with unhealthy vices.[43]

Worry is often used to avoid stronger negative feelings. For example, instead of feeling hurt or sad by something a friend did, you may lean more toward feeling anxious or worried because that feeling is easier to deal with. Worry is also often used as a buffer. If you're always waiting for the negative outcome, then you won't be hurt as badly if the negative outcome happens. Staying in a constant low-level state of negativity protects you from a crushing letdown when a positive outcome doesn't occur.[44] When applying for jobs, it can often be an arduous process of many applications, resumes, and interviews. If you assume that you won't get the job during the process, it won't hurt as much if you don't get it. This is a defense mechanism that many people use but has no real benefit in the long run.

Worrying can also have a negative physical effect on the body. Worry, which is mental, leads to stress, which is physical. Stress releases hormones into your brain that can cause brain mass and IQ to diminish. It also increases the likelihood of heart disease, cancer, premature aging, clinical depression, dementia, and Alzheimer's disease.[45] With all these negatives attached to worrying, it is vital to learn how to focus on things you *can* control and let go of the things you *can't.*

As a basketball coach, I constantly struggled with how little was in my control. A considerable amount of a game results from players, referees, opponents, and luck. Even though I knew this, I couldn't let go, and that created massive anxiety. I ruminated over things I couldn't change or affect. I lost sleep and peace of mind. It wasn't until I began to really understand, internalize, and focus on what I could control that my anxiety started to dissipate. That didn't happen until a year or so after I stepped away from coaching basketball. But that understanding has allowed me to pursue new endeavors with a more productive mindset.

How I Began to Understand What I Could Control

Learning to understand and focus only on what you can control can be a difficult and frustrating process. By no means have I perfected it, but there is no doubt that I have grown by leaps and bounds. I absolutely did not figure this out on my own and it did not happen overnight. I have had more than a few teachers, but two that really struck a chord with me were Ryan Holiday and the U.S. Military.

Ryan Holiday is much accomplished but is most famous for his speaking and writing about stoicism. He has written multiple books and spoken to numerous professional sports teams, corporations, and the military. I discovered his books and the philosophy of stoicism a couple years after experiencing the height of my anxiety and panic. Once I learned about it, my life changed forever.

Stoicism in its simplest form is a philosophy of understanding that we don't control the events that happen to us. Instead, we control how we respond to those events. We can't choose how people act or what happens to us, but we do control what *we* will do. Once I began to internalize this, I understood that my focus didn't need to be on everything that was going on around me. Instead, I needed to focus on what I could do. I don't control what people think of me as a coach or a person. All I can control is who I am, what I think, and what actions I take. After that, I let the rest fall into place.

There are a number of different U.S. military sources that helped to teach me to focus only on what I can control. There are too many to name them all. But one that comes to mind is U.S. Navy SEAL Rob O'Neill. Among many of the heroic things he has done, he is most famous for shooting and killing Osama Bin Laden. During an interview he mentioned multiple times that he was able to focus on what he could control on the Bid Laden raid.

- They had to fly into the compound in Pakistan. At any point they could have been shot out of the sky, but he couldn't worry about that. It would have been a waste of energy and he had zero effect on whether it happened or not.
- While flying into the compound, one of the helicopters crashed, they were left with only one of two working helicopters with which to get out of there. But he couldn't focus on that because he had a mission to complete.
- Because of the helicopter crash he wasn't able to enter the house at the location where he had practiced for weeks. Unable to enter from the roof, he couldn't worry that the plan had changed.
- They had to fly out of the Pakistani compound when they completed the mission. They faced the same risk of being shot down. He couldn't worry about that because he could not control that risk.[46]

If Rob or any of the other SEALs focused on parts of that mission that were outside of their control, it could have been disastrous. I have not been put into that stressful or dangerous of a situation. But if the

Seals can learn to focus only on what they can control in their environment, surely, I can learn to pay more attention to what I can control in mine.

What We Can Control

There are only two things we have absolute control over: our thoughts and our actions in the moment. We may be able to influence other outcomes, but we can fully control only those two things and nothing else.

Thoughts

You control what goes on in your head. That doesn't mean you won't have negative thoughts. But you do choose whether or how long those thoughts stay in your mind. With time and effort, you can teach yourself how to stay focused on the positive and constructive in any situation.

Picture a bucket. That bucket represents your mind. Now picture that bucket filled to the brim with dirty water. The dirty water represents all those negative thoughts filling up your mind. Now place the bucket under a faucet and add a little bit of clean water. At first, it's mostly the clean water on top that spills over, leaving you still with a bucketful of dirty water. But if you continue to pour more and more clean water into the bucket, most of the dirty water will eventually flush out. This is what happens when you fill your mind with positive thoughts. Eventually the undesirable thoughts are replaced with constructive ones.

Here's the most important part. If you let that clean water just sit without continuing to add more clean water, it'll eventually get dirty again. You want to add positive thoughts constantly to your brain to keep things from turning negative again.

Actions

You have control over your actions. You can choose to take the necessary steps to reach your goals or choose to sit on the couch all day binge-watching the latest Netflix series. You can choose to stay after practice and work on your jump shot for another thirty minutes or choose to go home and play video games. You can choose to react poorly when the coach takes you out of the game or you can choose to respond graciously and encourage your teammates.

Every single action has consequences. Often when people hear the word "consequences," they think of something negative. But sometimes the consequences are good. If you work out regularly and eat healthy, the consequences are going to be that your body feels good, and you will most likely have fewer health issues. But if you sit around all day and eat fast food, your body will develop numerous health problems rather quickly. Before you do or don't do something, keep in mind there will be some type of consequence.

The idea that you have complete control over your actions massively influences your ability to be a disciplined person and reach your goals. Too often people let how they *feel* in that moment dictate their actions. If you do this, you most likely won't get too much accomplished in your life, as it is not often that we *feel* like doing difficult things, even when we know it is good for us or is helping us to achieve a goal that we know we want.

Here's the trick that almost all successful people know and understand that help them to reach amazing heights. Very rarely are you going to *want* to do it. Do it anyway! The very fact that it is difficult or tiring means that it's most likely not fun and exciting. Do it anyway. Your feelings don't have control over your actions. You do!

Working Through Pressure

It is normal to feel a certain level of pressure during a game or performance. The level of importance you and others place upon the event can change from day to day, hour to hour, minute to minute. Learning to work through pressure situations is often the difference between wins and losses, success, or failure.

A study was published in 2011 that analyzed the effects of psychological pressure on NBA players shooting free throws during the 2002-2003 through 2009-2010 seasons. In a pressure situation, such as making a game winning free throw with little time left on the clock, players made roughly 7 percent fewer free throws than usual. Even Michael Jordan, the consensus greatest basketball player of all time, shot a lower free-throw percentage in the waning moments of important games.[47] One could argue that this difference results from playing on the road. But an analysis that included more than 440 NBA players and 340,000 free throws found that the home team actually shot a lower percentage from the free throw line in the final minutes. The visiting team shot roughly the same percentage.[48]

Why do NBA players tend to shoot a lower percentage in the critical moments? They could be focusing on the pressure of the situation and other elements out of their control, such as the opinion of others, commotion in the stands, a remark made by an opponent trying to get under their skin, or a missed call by a referee. In situations like these, athletes often overthink the execution of movements they've practiced many times. When that happens, the movement doesn't flow as seamlessly, and mistakes happen. But if they could focus on what's within their control, such as their pre-shot routine and staying in the moment, they would have a higher rate of success. This is easier said than done and even more so when in high stress situations. That's why it's important to practice this mindfulness when the pressure is low.

Things You Can Control as an Athlete

People can be quick to point fingers elsewhere when something doesn't go their way. Fortunately, there are elements an athlete or performer can completely control. By taking control of these elements, you'll be eliminating excuses for why you didn't perform at your best. By focusing on these elements, you can take more control of your performance and silence much of the chatter in your mind that is caused by your Inner Rival. Many people often don't take full control of these factors, which keeps them from performing at their peak. Focusing on what you can control will take your abilities to the next level:

Attitude – You choose whether to have a negative or positive attitude. You have control over what you focus on and how you talk to others. You don't have to be happy and cheery all the time, but don't let the

Inner Rival's negative voice take control and steer the ship. When you notice a negative attitude bubbling up, change it to a constructive one. Your attitude also impacts those around you and is actually contagious.

The late Pat Summit is one of the most highly decorated NCAA basketball coaches of all-time, with 7 NCAA Coach of the Year awards and 8 NCAA National Championships. She achieved numerous conference titles and other awards in her time coaching the University of Tennessee woman's basketball team. She developed her own coaching philosophy that she called "The Definite Dozen." One of those dozens was, "Handle success like you handle failure." She understood that you had control over your attitude and how you handle success and failure. It is important you don't let the outcome of an event control how you feel or what you think. That choice is yours.

Fitness – You have full control of your fitness level, barring injury and illness. In your sport there's a certain fitness level you should attain to be competitive. If you're not at that level, it is 100 percent up to you to get there. No one can improve your fitness level but you. In the offseason you can make massive improvements to your fitness level. It's not easy and usually not fun, but you have the choice to put in the time and energy to be at a high level of fitness.

Effort – Only you can decide how hard you need to try and what a full level of effort is for you. You can convince everyone that you're trying your hardest, but only you know if you're giving it your all. And that means something different for everyone.

Just because you're practicing more or performing better than someone else, doesn't mean you're doing *your* best. While at the same time, just because someone is practicing more or performing better than you, doesn't mean you're *not* doing your best.

Rest & Recovery – If you're an active person who is struggling to focus and give a full effort, there's a good chance it's because you aren't giving your mind and body enough time to rest and recover. When you push yourself outside of your comfort zone, you need to give yourself time to recover both physically and mentally. Make sure you aren't pushing too hard or letting yourself be pulled in too many directions. You need time to mentally and physically recharge.

Nutrition – You're in charge of what goes into your body. Good in, good out. Bad in, bad out. It can be that simple. It's important to treat your body well by giving it the right fuel for ample energy. Your nutrition has a huge effect on your focus and energy. Be mindful of what you put inside of yourself.

Communication – Many mistakes and errors, in both sports and life, can be avoided if people communicate effectively. Good communication requires both clear speaking and good listening. Take the time to communicate to those around you and listen to what they have to say. Along my coaching journey, I often told our players, "It's very difficult to over-communicate." I believe that is true for most situations in life.

Preparation – You have full control over how much you prepare for the situations you'll face in life. Whether you're getting ready for a game, presentation, or job interview, the amount of time and effort you spend preparing is completely within your control. Ninety percent of our success is in the preparation. Never wing it or cheat on the pre-work.

Reaction/Response – You don't always have control of the things that happen to and around you. You do have control over how you react or respond. Whether it's a bad call by a ref, trash talk by opponents or fans, or a change in the weather, you choose how you'll react or respond to that adversity. As stated earlier in the book, the practice of meditation can be helpful in developing the ability to choose the way you want to respond.

Focus – A multitude of messages may pop in and out of your head, but *you* get to decide which of them to focus on. Don't allow your focus to attach to negative thoughts that only bring you down. Let those go and replace them with more productive thoughts.

Body Language – Your body language is one of the strongest communicators you have. Often your body tells the world what you're thinking whether you want it to or not. Do your best to make sure you're carrying yourself with confidence and strength no matter the situation. The choice is yours!

Nate Ebner is a former professional football player for the New England Patriots and a former player on the US Olympic rugby team. In his book *Finish Strong*, he describes how he was able to control the controllable and achieve such amazing feats.

"Even before training camp started, I knew I'd need to learn the language of Patriots football. Literally. The verbiage they used to describe things in the defensive and special teams meeting rooms was unique. The Patriots had their own language. It was sort of a parallel to English.

I made two hundred flash cards to deal with that. Each card had the Patriots jargon on one side and what it meant on the other. All summer before camp started, I studied those cards like they were the Bible, because in some very tangible way, they were. If the Pats cut me, it would not be because I was too lazy to learn the language.

If they decided I wasn't big/fast/strong enough, OK. The NFL is full of physical freaks. I can't control that. Knowing the playbook was something I could control".[49]

The following exercises will help you control the controllable:

Exercise 1

Draw two circles that overlap in the middle. In the first circle, write "Things that matter" and list things important to you. In the second circle, write "Things I can control" and list things you can control. In the section in the middle of the two circles write "Things I should focus on." That section should be filled with both things you can control and that matter to you. That is the sweet spot. You want to spend your time focusing on things that matter and are also within your control.

Exercise 2

Here is an exercise I like to do with younger athletes to help demonstrate what they have control over.

- Try to control anything in the past.
- Try and control something in the future.

What you will find is that you can't control either. You can only control what you think and do right now! Though this exercise can seem slightly childish, I feel like it is a great way to remind myself what I can control when I find myself worrying about things outside of my control.

Chapter 5

GET OUT OF
YOUR COMFORT ZONE

From 1886 to 1954, countless athletes tried to run a mile in under four minutes to no avail. Some came to believe it was physically impossible to do. Experts believed it could only be accomplished on a day that was 68 degrees with no wind, on a track that was hard/dry clay, and in front of a huge crowd for the energy. That is until May 6, 1954. On a cold, rainy day in front of a crowd of a few thousand, Rodger Bannister broke through the four-minute mile barrier with a blazing speed of 3:59.30 minutes.

Amazingly, just 46 days later, it was broken again by a runner named John Landy. He ran it at a pace of 3:57.9 minutes. Since then, thousands more have broken the barrier, and pushed it to the current world record time of 3:43.13 (at the time this book was written).[50]

Your Inner Rival

Your Inner Rival wants to keep you in your comfort zone where you know it's safe. When you leave your comfort zone, you might encounter painful, difficult, or stressful situations. Your Inner Rival will say things like "you're too tried," "there's no need to work that hard," or "the bed feels really comfortable." Your Inner Rival wants you to stay in your comfort zone where there are no surprises.

What your Inner Rival doesn't understand is that if you want to achieve anything great, you must get out of your comfort zone. Pushing yourself out of your comfort zone is not as bad as your Inner Rival will tell you. Yes, it can be difficult. Yes, it's uncomfortable. But that's what it takes to achieve something amazing and be who Teddy Roosevelt referred to as "The Man in the Arena".[51] It beats the heck out of the alternative—being average.

Introduction

Our modern society continually tries to make things easier, faster, and more convenient. We hardly need to leave our houses anymore. We can get meals and groceries delivered. We can access music, thousands of movies, books, and other entertainment at the click of a button. We can video call anyone around the world in an instant. Paradoxically, these revolutionary products and services designed to keep people in their comfort zones were invented and developed by people pushing themselves out of their comfort zones.

What is the "comfort zone?" It's a "behavioral space where your activities and behaviors fit a routine and pattern that minimize stress and risk, providing a state of mental security. You benefit in obvious ways: regular happiness, low anxiety, and reduced stress".[52] That doesn't sound so bad. But if you stay in your comfort zone, you will never be able to reach your full potential!

Psychologists Robert M. Yerkes and John D. Dodson have discovered that to *maximize* performance you need a level of *optimal arousal*.[53] Optimal arousal is different for everyone and depends on the situation. It's based just outside of *your* comfort zone. Too much arousal or stimulus will cause your performance to suffer. But insufficient arousal or stimulus will create boredom.[54] The key is to push yourself just outside of your comfort zone to maximize your performance. Your body and mind will adapt to what you do, so you'll need to push yourself a bit more as you grow and improve. Begin by slowly pushing yourself to the point where you feel uncomfortable in order to find what works best for you.

Yerkes and Dodson were among the first to test the connection between arousal and performance. They did this by placing mice in a maze and seeing how quickly they finished. When a small electric shock was administered, the mice completed the maze at a faster pace than when no shock was used. The shock pushed them out of their comfort zone. When the shock became too strong, the mice chose to hide rather than finish the maze. This was how Yerkes and Dodson discovered the *optimal arousal* or "Goldilocks" zone.[55] They weren't too comfortable, and they weren't too far out of their comfort zone, but right in the sweet spot to maximize output.

When you stretch a rubber band and then let go, it will fly forward. When you stretch it back just enough it will fly a good distance. But if you stretch the rubber band back too far, it'll snap. The same thing goes for your attempts to get out of your comfort zone. When you push yourself the right amount, you will flourish and grow. But if you find that you are pushing yourself too far out of your comfort zone you will eventually snap. That is why finding the "Goldilocks zone" is key. That's where you'll maximize your growth without snapping and quitting.

Comfort Zone and the Great Barrier Reef

Motivational author Earl Nightingale described the Great Barrier Reef along the northeastern coast of Australia. It is lifeless and boring on the lagoon side and vibrant, alive, and energetic on the ocean side.[56] There's no stress or arousal on the lagoon side to challenge the reef and help it flourish. It becomes bored and stale. But the side of the reef that faces the ocean is continually challenged. It thrives, in those uncomfortable conditions. Like the reef, we need to have an optimal level of stress and challenge to keep us vibrant.

Think back to a time you achieved something special or meaningful to you. Did you get pushed outside of what felt comfortable? Did you run into challenges and obstacles that you had to overcome? I bet you did. That's a major reason why it feels special to you. The fact that you had to push yourself until you were uncomfortable *is* a large part of why the achievement is special to you. If an achievement feels easy, it usually doesn't feel as gratifying as when you are able to silence your Inner Rival and move into uncharted waters.

Getting Uncomfortable Can Create Better Learning

Putting yourself in an uncomfortable situation is just as it sounds: uncomfortable. But science is beginning to show we may actually learn more when we're uncomfortable. In a study conducted in 2003, monkeys were given juice as a reward for hitting specific targets. When the monkeys could predict when they would receive the juice, the areas of the brain associated with learning essentially shut down. But when the monkeys were unable to predict what would happen, those areas of the brain lit up.[57] Their minds were working to figure out a pattern for when and why they would get the rewards.

This study demonstrates that when we get out of our comfort zone, we continue to adapt, grow, and figure things out. That's how we continue to innovate as a society. We look for challenges that push us outside of our comfort zone, achieve it, then look for the next challenge to motivate us. Without that desire to seek out new challenges, innovations like the car, airplane, or cellphone wouldn't exist.

Comfort Zone and Weightlifting

If you do the exact same workout every time, your improvement will eventually flatten out and plateau. To grow continually, you need to change things by adding more weight, repetitions, sets, days of the week, or even decrease time between sets. When physically pushing yourself past your comfort level, your Inner Rival will scream at you to stop. But the only way to grow when lifting weights and improving your fitness is to make it more difficult than the last time you worked out. When pushing past that point of comfort, your Inner Rival begins to tell you to quit. That's the point when you improve the process of silencing your Inner Rival.

Getting out of your comfort zone physically isn't the only way to practice getting uncomfortable. You can do it in a multitude of different areas. It just depends on where, as a person, you want to grow. I truly believe that there is something to be learned by pushing yourself physically past your comfort zone on a regular basis. When you do, it begins to bleed into all areas of your life. You may find that getting out of your comfort zone and expanding your life are quite as difficult as you may have thought.

The 1 Percent Rule – Compound Effect

To see these gains, you don't need to push yourself *so* hard every time that you feel like you want to quit. You can actually make massive progress over time with simple, small gains each day. This is what's known as the compound effect or the 1 Percent Rule. If you can get yourself to improve by just 1 percent each day, then mathematically you would be 37x better than you were a year ago. Obviously, this isn't an exact rule, as most things can't be measured with a precise percentage. But the 1 Percent Rule is a great reminder to us that a little extra effort each day goes a long way. Continual small steps can compound upon one another to make massive progress.

Here is an example of how to apply the 1 Percent Rule. The amount of recovery time a professional bodybuilder takes is crucial for the body to grow and repair itself after the stress from lifting weights. Sleep is an extremely important piece to the recovery program.

Imagine a weightlifter deciding to sleep thirty minutes more each night. Thirty minutes more per night doesn't sound like much, but when you compound it over 365 days, that turns into 182 more hours of sleep. That can make a huge difference in a bodybuilder's recovery process.

The 1 Percent Rule is also helpful with improving mental strength. In looking back at our chapter on meditation, it can be a difficult practice to building into your routine, especially if you try starting off meditating with as much as fifteen to thirty minutes a day right away. Instead, start small with one minute a day, then add another minute the next day, and another the next. After ten days, you'll be up to ten minutes of meditation a day. Because you have slowly built the practice into your routine rather than diving in headfirst, it'll be easier to maintain. If that still feels like too much too handle, break it down into even smaller increments. The idea is just that you improve and add a bit more each time. Continual progress is the key.

Get Comfortable Being Uncomfortable

Nothing impressive or amazing has ever been achieved by someone who was content being comfortable. Those achievements are reserved for people who are comfortable with being uncomfortable. You need to get yourself to the point where you don't mind a little discomfort. You don't mind because you know it won't last forever and it will be beneficial in the long run. A great way to get used to a bit of discomfort is to do something every day that makes you feel uncomfortable. The more you do it, the less dramatic it will feel.

If you never push yourself to the point of feeling discomfort, it will feel very dramatic if you are ever forced to. By continually learning to push yourself to the point of discomfort you will be amazed how resilient you are and how much your mind and body can handle.

Navy SEALs become experts at rising to the occasion in the midst of discomfort. As part of their Basic Underwater Demolition/ SEALS training, the recruits are continually told to turn into "sugar cookies." They must get wet and sandy from head to toe. This creates chafing and eventually turns the skin raw and bleeding. They're learning and practicing getting comfortable with discomfort. This is a crucial skill because they never know what kind of terrible conditions or situations they may encounter on their missions. They need to know that they will be prepared to continue the mission until the end no matter what happens.

Being comfortable in situations that are uncomfortable is one of the most important skills you can develop on the way to silencing your Inner Rival. Make sure you are getting out of your comfort zone every day.

Perceived Limits – 40 Percent Rule

David Goggins is a former Navy SEAL, ultramarathon runner, author, entrepreneur, and former Guinness

World Record holder for most pull-ups of 4,030 in 24 hours. He made popular the 40 Percent Rule.[58] Goggins teaches that when you reach the point of seeming exhaustion in any activity, you have actually used only about 40 percent of what your body and mind can produce. The next 60 percent is willpower. This is a concept that many in the military learn about themselves.

When most people reach their uncomfortable threshold, their Inner Rivals tells them, "That's enough for the day and never push through that discomfort." When the warriors, champions, and elite performers hit that discomfort zone, they realize it's only a mental barrier and push through. Top performers in any field are able to push that pain threshold further away and see how far they can go.

This is a tool that you can use to measure your effort and assess how hard you're working. Think of the 40 Percent Rule as your comfort zone. You need to push yourself out of that 40 percent zone to see real improvement and be able to grow. Don't try to get to 100 percent every time, because if you do, you'll drain the tank. Push yourself to where you want to quit and then go a bit further. Prove to yourself you're stronger than your Inner Rival. Don't let it dictate when your work is done. You choose that yourself!

Embrace the Suck

I have gained so much from learning about the mindset and training that goes into building the amazing warriors within our military's special operations units. Brent Gleeson is a Navy SEAL and author of the book, *Embrace the Suck*. This is another mindset and mantra the SEALs use to help them push through challenges. If you want to grow and achieve something amazing, you're going to have to go through things you don't enjoy. You can either 1) whine and complain about how hard it is, which will make it feel even more difficult and most likely lead to you giving up or 2) embrace the suck and push forward.

In life, there are always going to be challenges you don't want to endure and tasks you don't want to do. Here's what Gleason writes about embracing the suck:

> Becoming more resilient starts with changing your perspective on adversity. Pain can in fact be transformed into a useful energy force for accomplishing great feats. For gaining perspective. For building physical and emotional resilience. When you can master the ability to control pain whatever form it comes in—and even lean into it, it doesn't have to hurt so badly.[59]

I've always used fitness as a way to work on embracing the suck. I'm not Mr. Olympia, but I've made an effort to stay in shape over the years. As I've learned more about this mindset, I've enjoyed challenging myself with difficult workouts even more. On Memorial Day of 2021, I did my first "Murph" workout. This workout is very popular in the CrossFit and SEAL community and was created in memory of Navy Lt. Michael Murphy who died in Afghanistan on June 28, 2005. This workout consists of running one mile, 100 pull-ups, 200 push-ups, 300 body squats, and then running one more mile. It was extremely difficult, but it felt good knowing I could push myself through the pain and finish my challenge.

Friends and I also did a Tough Mudder obstacle course that included a ten-mile run and twenty-six obstacles through mud, dirt, and water. I was bleeding and cramping at the end, but I finished! Those may not be the most difficult tasks in the world, but they pushed me outside of my comfort zone and built up my confidence.

Growth Is in the Boring

You can find motivation from a variety of sources. I love to hear and read stories about people who achieve amazing feats or are genius in their work ethic. Kobe Bryant was one of those people. There are so many stories about Kobe and the amount of time and effort he put into his game as well as other areas of his life. My favorite Kobe Bryant story was written by an athletic trainer named Rob who worked with Kobe while he played for Team USA Basketball:

> "As the USA basketball team was preparing to play in the London Olympics, Kobe called Rob, the team trainer, in his hotel room at 4:15 a.m. to see if he would work him out. Rob obliged and met Kobe at the facility as soon as he could. When Rob showed up around five o'clock, Kobe was already in a full sweat from working out. For the next seventy-five minutes, they did conditioning drills. After that, they did

another forty-five minutes of strength training exercise in the weight room. When they were done, Kobe went to practice his shot, and Rob went back to his hotel room to get some much-needed sleep. He had to be back at the gym for practice at Noon.

When Rob returned to the gym, he found Kobe already there shooting in a corner by himself.

Rob went up to Kobe and asked, 'So when did you finish?'

'Finish what?'

'Getting your shots up. What time did you leave the facility?'

'Oh, just now. I wanted eight-hundred makes so yeah, just now'".[60]

This story demonstrates Kobe's work ethic. If you want to be great at anything, from athletics to music to business, you'll have to work long, hard hours. And those hours can get really boring. But working through the boring is where growth takes place.

Kobe spent many hours working on his conditioning, strength, and skillset before even starting team practice for the day. On top of that, he worked out this way all year round for years. I promise you he got bored at some point during all of those hours in the gym. But he knew if he wanted to become the greatest basketball player on the planet, he was going to have to put in more time and effort than anyone else. Kobe understood that he had to work through the boring. That is what he did.

His time and effort were even more special because he didn't just mindlessly work through the hours. He put in *deliberate practice* hours (see below) during that time. He focused on breaking down his skills and trying to perfect the nuances of each one. He paid attention to his successes and failures and then made adjustments. He found different skills to build and ways to train. He even built meditation into his training routine and learned to focus on being in the moment and mindful while training. That's what separated Kobe from the rest.

Another amazing athlete with stories of a strong work ethic and hours of unseen effort is Michael Phelps. As mentioned in the previous chapter, his unbelievable achievements in swimming have awarded him a total of twenty-eight Olympic medals with twenty-three of them being gold. During that time, he trained for five consecutive years without a day off. There were no birthdays, holidays, or vacations without daily training built into the schedule.[61] There is no doubt that there was some boredom in those five years. But Phelps persisted.

Are you willing to work and stay focused during the long unseen hours to achieve your goals?

Deliberate Practice

Deliberate practice is a major key to improvement. Over the years, I've spent hundreds of hours watching athletes shoot hoops, play tennis, and workout on their own. Very few of them work with *deliberate* practice. Most of the time they were doing what I call "social shooting." They were shooting around with teammates or by themselves while sort of mindlessly going through the motions, or in the weight room doing the workout half-heartedly. They weren't paying attention to what they were doing correctly or incorrectly. They were just doing. There's definitely a time to mess around with friends and have fun but if you *really* want to improve your game, you must practice with a purpose.

It's not necessarily easy to practice this way. It can get uncomfortable because you have to be completely honest with yourself about what and how you're doing, which requires you to get out of your comfort zone. There are three parts to deliberate practice that you will want to focus on. Missing any one of them will drastically lower the return of investment on your time during the practice.

Purpose

You know there's a reason for why and what you're doing in practice. There's a purpose for putting in the time to develop that move, shot, or skill. You're breaking down the different elements of the skill and focusing on doing them correctly. You have a reason for why you are working on what you are working on. You're not just doing something just to do it.

As a coach I often ask my players, "Why did you make that decision?" When they response, "I don't know," that is one of my biggest pet peeves. I ask this question not because I'm irritated, but because I'm curious. If I can understand their thinking, I can help teach them to make more productive decisions or help them to see other options. If you, the athlete, don't know why you're doing something, then why do it?

That is the opposite of deliberate practice! Always have a reason or a purpose for doing something.

Feedback

Acting upon the feedback and correcting yourself can be uncomfortable. You must admit to yourself that you did something incorrectly, are confused, or don't understand. For most people, that can be a shot to the ego. When the ego is hurt, you're out of your comfort zone. When that feeling happens, remember that feedback is important and that success lies outside of your comfort zone.

Pay attention to feedback and make the necessary changes. This rule applies whether it's your own feedback from your success and mistakes or feedback from coaches. I've seen too many athletes receive feedback but then continue mindlessly to do the same unproductive thing over and over again. That's the exact opposite of deliberate practice.

Time

As I've already emphasized, you must put in the time working on your game. It often frustrated me when players attended team practices but did not put in any extra time working on their game. They wondered why they did not improve at the rate they wanted. If you want to be great, you need to understand that it is uncommon to be great. You must put in an uncommon number of hours to get there.

That is true no matter what you want to achieve! You need to put in the time to improve, whether as a speaker, teacher, tennis player, salesperson, or parent. It takes time to be great!

The Ten Thousand Hour Rule, made popular by the author Malcolm Gladwell, provides a good reference point for the amount of deliberate practice time you require to become proficient. Ten thousand hours isn't an exact number, but if you put in those hours of deliberate practice, you're well on your way to becoming great in the area you pursue.

Kobe is a great example of someone who used deliberate practice perfectly. He explained his deliberate practice routine when discussing a game in which he scored 81 points. Kobe would make thousands of shots in the offseason. He worked through actions and shots from his team's offense that he would later take during games. He was trying to simulate what he was going to encounter when competing against future opponents. He wanted his body and muscles to know exactly what they were expected to do in the future.[62] Kobe understood the keys to deliberate practice. He had a purpose, paid attention to feedback, and put in the time. He knew that was the fastest way to improve.

A 2007 *Harvard Business Review* article, "The Making of an Expert," talked about how it's not necessarily the amount of time working on a skill that creates the expert, but the amount of effort that creates that expert:

"The journey to truly superior performance is neither for the faint of heart nor for the impatient. The development of genuine expertise requires struggle, sacrifice, and honest, often painful self-assessment. There are no shortcuts. It will take you at least a decade to achieve expertise, and you will need to invest that time wisely, by engaging in "deliberate" practice—practice that focuses on tasks beyond your current level of competence and comfort. You will need a well-informed coach not only to guide you through deliberate practice but also to help you learn how to coach yourself".[63]

Getting out of your comfort zone doesn't mean just physical hard work. It also means mentally and emotionally working past what's comfortable. Deliberate practice is more about getting out of your mental comfort zone than it is about your physical comfort zone. Staying focused, working on your craft correctly, and being honest with yourself are all important parts of deliberate practice.

Your Inner Rival will continue to do whatever it can to keep you in your comfort zone because that's where you know you're safe. But it's not where you'll grow. Silence your Inner Rival and learn to push yourself past what you thought possible. You'll be amazed at what you can accomplish when you quiet that voice and stretch yourself to your limits.

The following exercises will help you to get out of your comfort zone:

1. *Learn something new* – By learning something new, you are putting yourself in a position to have to fail and learn, which is often an uncomfortable feeling. This is a great way to push yourself outside of your comfort zone. It doesn't have to be anything drastic, or even related to a field in which you are already experienced

2. *Talk to a stranger while waiting in line or for an appointment* – For many people, striking up a conversation with a random stranger can be an excruciatingly awkward encounter. By putting yourself into those situations where you feel uncomfortable but don't have anything to lose if the conversation goes south, you will improve your ability to handle uncomfortable situations with more grace.

3. *Volunteer to be a leader of a group at school or work.* – By putting yourself in a leadership role, you are taking on accountability for what happens in that group. It's your job to make sure everyone is on the same page and moving in the same direction. This can force you to make difficult decision or have difficult conversations. You will have to solve problems and be creative. All these situations help to increase your comfort zone.

Chapter 6
PERCEPTION

*There is an ancient fable about a
farmer in a small village:*

*One day the farmer's only horse ran away.
Upon hearing the news, his neighbors
came over and said, 'We are sorry to hear,
that is such bad luck.'*

'We'll see,' the farmer replied.

*The next day the horse returned, bringing
along with it three more wild horses.*

*'How amazing!' the neighbors exclaimed.
'Your horse returned and brought along with
it three more horses! You are so fortunate!'*

'We'll see,' replied the farmer again.

*The following day, his son tried to ride one of
the wild horses and was thrown off. When he
landed, his leg was broken. Once they heard
the news, the neighbors again came to offer
their sympathy. 'Now your son cannot help on
the farm. What bad luck you're having!'*

'We'll see,' said the farmer.

*A week later, the military came through the
village drafting every healthy young man
for the war. They passed by the farmer's son
because of his broken leg. It was a terrible war
where almost everyone died. The neighbors*

came over and told the farmer,
'What great luck that your son
didn't have to fight in the war!'

Again, the farmer replied, 'We'll see'

Inner Rival

Your Inner Rival will make you think that situations are more dangerous or difficult than they actually are by showing you all the potential negative outcomes and hiding the positive ones. This false reality clouds your perception, making you feel stressed, anxious, nervous, and fearful. It creates a perception that is not true.

Growing your awareness about the ways you perceive events and stressors gives you a significant advantage. You'll have more confidence and better control of your mindset. It won't be easy. You'll have to put yourself in uncomfortable situations. But we already know that is a good thing from the previous chapter. When you understand that you choose the meaning of everything that happens in your life, you will learn to use your perception to your advantage. You will take positive steps toward silencing your Inner Rival.

Perceptions

An event, in and of itself, doesn't have universal meaning. It's up to the individual and their perception of said event that gives the event its meaning. As each event unfolded for the farmer, the neighbors had their own immediate interpretations about it being good or bad. But the farmer understood that life's events aren't that cut and dried. He understood each event could be interpreted multiple ways depending on each person's perception and life experiences. He also understood that perceptions can change with the passage of time as well.

Perception is the process of becoming aware of something through our senses. Our sensory receptors (smell, taste, sight, touch, and hearing) take in the information, which gets transmitted to our brain. Our brains then unconsciously categorize the stimuli, so we can make sense of it and understand what's going on around us. We then interpret that information based on our perceptions and experiences. This process happens hundreds of thousands of times a day, which allows us to navigate daily life without being overwhelmed.[64] The phenomenon has a profound impact on how we interpret life's events.

How Do You Form Your Perceptions?

Since perceptions are critical to how life's events are viewed, you want to learn to use perception to your advantage. This requires an understanding of how perceptions are formed. According to psychologist and life coach Dr. Linda Humphreys, "our past experiences greatly influence how we decode things. Certain people, things, and situations can trigger you to interpret things through a positive or negative lens based on those past experiences. The totality of your perceptions—regarding yourself, your life, life in general, others, and so on—creates and impacts your personal reality and ultimately your experience of life".[65] Additional factors, such as your education, faith, culture, and values, come into play and create your life experiences.

Everything you go through in life builds upon past perceptions. Each person's perception of the same event can be and often are different. Many of us take in the same movies, songs, books, etc. but we don't all feel the same way about them. Some people hear rap music and love the lyrics and beat, while others find it obscene and filled with foul language. Many people enjoy romantic comedies where there is always a happy ending, while others think those are boring and unrealistic. This goes for any of our other physical experiences as well. What we like to eat, drink, listen to, and so much more is based on our perceptions created over time.

Our perceptions are also impacted by fear, stress, anxiety, happiness, and other emotions rooted in past experiences. Preparing to deliver a speech can bring a wide range of emotions. One person may love it, while another is absolutely terrified of speaking in front of others. This difference is most likely because of past experiences they either interpreted as a success or disaster. If past speeches have gone well, then chances are you won't be dreading the next one. If you made mistakes or interpreted a previous talk as poor, there's a good chance you'll be more nervous for the next one. The good news is you have the ability to change how you perceive the events you experience. We'll dive into that idea deeper later in the chapter.

There are times when you may feel fear or anxiety in an event that is new to you. In the first time ever giving a speech, it is possible to be nervous and anxious even though you have never experienced a negative outcome for this type of event. That is normal. The desire to not screw up and feel ostracized from our "community" is built into our DNA, and our perception of doing something new is the desire to not make mistakes. That feeling of stress when doing something new, i.e., getting out of your comfort zone is completely natural. If you do have those feelings when doing something new, that is just your perception or your Inner Rival creating those negative thoughts. You have the ability to choose if you see a new event as exciting or if you allow the negative thoughts to take over.

Threat Response Verses Challenge Response

When faced with a potentially stressful situation, we automatically perceive it as a threat or challenge. Our appraisal is based on perceptions and past experiences. From those experiences, we unconsciously determine whether we have the ability to manage the event. We respond accordingly both psychologically and physiologically. This is the transactional model of stress and coping that is presented by Richard Lazarus and Susan Folkman in their book *Stress, Appraisal, and Coping.*[66] When determining whether we consider something a threat or challenge, our mind unconsciously and automatically asks two questions:

1. Could this situation cause harm or benefit?
2. Am I capable of handling the stressors of said situation?

Based on our unconscious answers, we go into either threat or challenge response. Rarely do we experience either one as 100 percent one way or another. Usually, our response is a combination of the two. It's the extent to which we experience each that's important.

Threat-Response

After determining something is a threat, our blood vessels begin to constrict (so that we won't bleed to death in case of injury). Blood flow to the brain decreases as it's needed for essential organs while in fight or flight mode. The adrenal gland begins to release cortisol, which increases blood sugar level and gives the body needed energy to either fight or flee. This makes the heart rate increase and blood pressure rise. Sensing threats also affects us mentally. Emotions turn negative. The ability to focus and make decisions becomes more difficult.[67] None of this is inherently bad if you are facing an immediate and life endangering threat. Only when the threat is imagined or chronic that it becomes a problem.

Whether the threats are real or imagined, your body will go through the same type of physical and mental response. When dealing with matters like competition, work deadlines, traffic, and tests, our life may not be in jeopardy, but our body and minds can react as if they are. Without the ability to process these perceived threats constructively, the effects of chronic stress can lead to health issues such as anxiety, depression, stroke, heart disease, and weight gain, among others.[68]

When I was having difficulty dealing with the emotions of coaching, my body was in constant threat response, which in turn created anxiety within me. Some of the issues that I experienced from this mindset I spoke about earlier. I felt nervous and anxious almost all the time. My mind would race. I would struggle to focus on what I was doing. Worst of all, I would beat myself up constantly with negative words and thinking. There was very little chance that I would be successful or even enjoy what I was doing while I had that mindset. It wasn't until I changed my perception of events and began to view difficult situations as a challenge rather than a threat that anxiety began to calm.

Challenge-Response

Your body and mind go through a different process once you establish that a particular situation or event is a challenge rather than a threat. It's a process that prepares you to handle and act upon the situation, not retreat from it like the threat response. Rather than constrict, blood vessels dilate, which allows for better blood flow and more oxygenated blood to the brain and muscles. Adrenal glands still release cortisol boosting energy, but hormone levels return to normal more quickly. The mindset stays more positive. Focus and coordination sharpen.[69] In athletics this happens all the time. It could be playing against a difficult opponent you have never beat, competing on a big stage that you haven't encountered before, being called on to take the game winning shot, or stepping up to bat with two outs in the bottom of the 9th inning. In all of these situations you choose if you fear failure or if you are ready to take on the challenge. Which mindset you choose will have massive effect on how your body and ability to focus respond. This response affects your chances of success.

When we deem something as a challenge rather than a threat, the stress we experience is typically acute or short term. When we believe it's a challenge, we also unconsciously believe we're equipped to handle the trials ahead. Once it's over, we can relax. In fact, acute stress has been shown to promote personal growth and myriad other health benefits.[70] But when we deem something to be a threat, the stress we experience can become chronic or long term if it's not processed correctly. Unless you are truly in a life-or-death situation, it's best if you can turn a perceived threat into a challenge. You do have the ability to choose how you're viewing the situation. Don't waste the power you have and allow your Inner Rival to choose your response for you

Perception and Stress

The negative impacts from stress wreak havoc on our world today. Some of the more recent statistics found by the American Institute of Stress include:[71]

- 77 percent of people experience stress that affects their health physically.
- 73 percent of people report that stress affects their health mentally.
- 48 percent of people stated stress was the reason for difficulty sleeping.

- The number one health concern for high school students is stress.
- 80 percent of people experience stress from work

Each of us experiences stress in our lives to some degree. How each one of us copes with, manages, experiences, or uses stress to our advantage is unique. For some the effects are more physical. For others they're more mental. Here are a few of the more common symptoms of stress and a rough percentage of people that report them:[72]

- Irritability and anger: 45 percent
- Fatigue or low energy: 41 percent
- Anxiety, nervousness or worry: 36 percent
- Feeling sad or depressed: 34 percent
- Muscle tension: 23 percent

Acute or short-term stress isn't necessarily a bad thing because our bodies are able to return to their natural state relatively quickly. Studies have shown that, similar to the personal growth that occurs when we go beyond our comfort zone, experiencing some stress can help us develop new abilities.[73] When stress turns long-term or chronic, considerable health issues arise.

Chronic stress has been connected to many of the leading causes of death in the US, such as heart disease, cancer, lung disease, and suicide. It's also a contributing factor in high blood pressure, anxiety, and depression. With stress being such an important topic today, the million-dollar question becomes, "How can you become better at working with your stress?" The answer is to change your perception!

Traffic, work deadlines, tough conversations with a friend or coworker, presentations, and tests are prime examples of stressful situations people face on a regular basis. None of these are threats to our actual safety but can stir up similar emotions and reactions within. To help eliminate or lessen some of the non-life-threatening stress, try to change your perception of the stress itself. Studies have shown that if you choose to believe stress, in and of itself, is good, your response to the stress is improved.[74] If you choose to believe stress is good for you, then it can be good. If you think it's bad for you, then it can be bad.

We can also choose to look at the stressful situation differently. Let's look at a few examples in which perception could change the view and effects of stress.

1. *Giving a presentation or speech* – According to the National Institutes of Mental Health, 75 percent of people rate public speaking as their number one fear.[75] Because this is a stressor for so many people, and nearly 100 percent of speeches aren't life threatening, the power to change the perception of giving a speech is quite beneficial. Try viewing it as an opportunity to share a topic that's important to you. It is also a chance to get out of your comfort zone and grow in an area you want to improve. If it's a sales pitch, look at it as a way to "win" the customer's business rather than a way to "lose" their business. If you perceive an upcoming speech as a positive and productive opportunity, you'll be in a better position to give a successful talk.

2. *Busy high school athlete or performer* – It's normal for many high school and college student athletes or performers to feel stressed by their numerous extracurricular obligations on top of academic, family, and social functions. With multiple activities to balance, the stress of thinking about everything can easily overwhelm even the most mentally tough. When this happens, the best thing to do is focus on what you can control in that moment. It can be easy to become swamped if you think about everything that needs to be done. Instead, view it as a challenge to focus on the moment. Focus on the task you are doing, when that one's done, move on to the next. This can help to elevate some of the stress that comes from an overcrowded schedule.

Perceptions and Performance

Perception influences nearly every aspect of sports and performance related activities. Choosing to accept a challenge and do your best, as opposed to letting the stress engulf your mind and emotions, will make a world of difference. Here are a few examples:

- *You show up to the soccer field, and it's a hundred degrees, humid, no wind, it feels like you could melt.* You can complain about the heat and that you don't like to play in that weather. Or you can also take it as a challenge to show your opponents that heat doesn't bother you. You can last in any weather. You don't even notice it!

- *You're watching your teammates run the basketball up and down the court, while sitting on the bench playing few, if any, minutes.* You can imagine all the possible reasons why the coach doesn't like you, plays favorites, and doesn't see how good you really are. Or you can talk to the coach, learn what you need to improve upon, ask questions, and work so hard they would be silly not to play you. Show them you are the best teammate around and will help the team in any way you can.
- *You have an important recital coming up to get into a good performing arts school.* You can worry about everything that could go wrong and the consequences if they do. You can focus on the pressure. You can obsess over how good everyone else is going to be. Or you can choose to focus on only the aspects of the performance that you can control and giving it your full effort.
- *You are facing the number one seed in an upcoming tournament.* You can ruminate over how good they are, how it's unfair that you must compete against them or that you don't stand a chance. Or you can view it as a challenge and an opportunity to test your skills. This is a time to show how good you are against the best!
- *You find out you must compete early in the day.* I would always hear a few players or parents make comments like, "I'm not good when I play in the morning." Or "It's too early for our boys to compete." When this mindset begins, it's just a way to make excuses if you don't play well. Both teams

are competing at the same time. Use it as a chance to show that it doesn't matter what time you participate. You'll always bring your best effort.

There are countless opportunities during competition and performance to work on the skill of creating perceptions that benefit you. It does take time and effort but the more you do it, the easier it gets. It doesn't guarantee a win or a perfect performance, but it gives you the best opportunity operate at your highest level. If the outcome doesn't go the way you want it to, you can still perceive the results in a way that helps you rather than one that tears down your confidence.

I still work constantly on changing my perception. At one point I started to realize how often I perceived something as unfair, too difficult, or a "threat" and how much of a negative impact those perceptions had on me mentally, emotionally, and even physically. I quickly started doing my best to change that viewpoint. I now view most situations as a challenge rather than a threat. I enjoy embracing a difficult situation. It's become a game within my mind to see if I can overcome whatever adversity is thrown my way. I still have much room for improvement. But I'm able to see and feel the continual progress that comes from silencing the Inner Rival and choosing the way I view situations.

Perception is *not* reality, but in a way it actually is. The way you perceive anything is *your* reality. That's an amazing power if used correctly. If you choose to perceive what happens to and around you in a negative light, it can hold you back. It'll disrupt the mindset needed to achieve the greatness within you. Do your best to find the challenge and positivity within any situation that arises, rather than focusing on the difficulty and risk of going for your dreams.

The following steps will help you improve your perception:

Meditate

By meditating, you'll be more in tune with your emotions, thoughts, and actions. You'll also become more aware of how you perceive the events happening to and around you. With that awareness, you can choose the way you want to view events. You'll look at issues more rationally, rather than letting a molehill turn into a mountain.

Challenge Your Current Perceptions

When events cause you to feel the emotional and physical reactions of threat-response, take the time to discern if that's the appropriate reaction. If it's not, try to change the way you're perceiving what's happening. By challenging your immediate reactions, you'll feel more control. You will be better equipped to respond to events in a way that's beneficial.

If Possible, Make Physical Changes to the Situation

There are times when you can make physical changes to the situation or environment to reduce stress or anxiety. For example, if you become anxious because of your commute to work or school, investigate other travel options. Maybe you can work from home a couple days a week or find a carpool buddy. If you become nervous before a game, try to modify your pregame routine to strengthen your mindset going into the competition. Sometimes a simple physical change can make all the difference in the world when it comes to your mindset.

Chapter 7
RESILIENCE

Louis Zamperini, American World War II Veteran and an Olympic distance runner, is one of the most resilient people to have ever walked the face of the earth. In 1934 as a high school track athlete, he set the state record for the mile run with a time of 4:21.3 minutes. He then went on to run in the 1936 Berlin Olympics in the 5000-meter race, where he placed 8th.

In 1941 Zamperini joined the Army Air Corps where he was trained as a bombardier. While flying a mission in 1934 his plane crashed in the Pacific Ocean, where they lost 5 of their 8 men aboard. The three survivors, one of whom was Zamperini, were in a lifeboat for nearly 30 days and ran out of food and water. While adrift in the ocean, they survived numerous shark attacks, chaotic weather, and air strikes from Japanese pilots.

The men were "rescued" by the Japanese military and were deemed prisoners of war. Because of his fame as an athlete Zamperini was treated extra harshly. Nearing starvation, he was forced to clean latrines and shovel coal while beaten constantly. Other soldiers and friends were forced to beat him as well.

He released was from the camp on September 5, 1945, more than two years after his plane went down. Zamperini went on to live another 69 years, passing away in July 2014 at the age of 97.

The Inner Rival

Your Inner Rival is constantly trying to persuade you to quit. When you're tired, it's the voice within saying, *"You've done enough for today. You should take a break."* Every time you fail, it's the voice saying, *"You should stop because it's not going to work anyway. It's too difficult"*. Your Inner Rival wants to keep you from trying and failing because it doesn't want you to know you can recover and bounce back. It doesn't want you to put in the effort to be great where there is a chance of failure because it wants you to believe that failure is fatal. Why get back up when you can just get knocked back down?

By strengthening your resilience, you'll find the obstacles and setbacks you face aren't quite as daunting as they initially appear. You'll understand that failure isn't final. It's just one step in the growing process. There's always a way to improve and a reason to keep going. You will learn that being a resilient person isn't something complicated. It really can be as simple as not giving up. Getting back up each time you get knocked down!

Introduction

I believe it's impossible to do anything amazing without facing and fighting through some type of adversity along the way. That's why resilience is so vital for success. Resilience is often considered one of the cornerstones to mental toughness. It's the ability to bounce back when faced with physical, mental, or emotional trauma. We all want to be considered resilient. But that requires going through difficult times, which people generally don't want to do.

Lucky for us, resilience is not something we're born with or without. It's learned and can be strengthened through challenge, tension, and adversity. It is just like any other skill or muscle. The problem most people experience when dealing with adversity is that they often make excuses, divert the blame, or quit. The only way to really be considered a resilient person is to face your fears, challenges, and doubts head on without quitting. Resilience doesn't mean you always win. It means you never give up.

While reading about resilient people and working to become more resilient myself, I enjoyed learning about Special Operators in our military, such as Navy SEALs, Delta Force, and Green Berets. These are some of the most resilient people on the planet. In order to get through their trainings, they must push themselves far beyond their perceived physical, emotional, and mental limits. They get less sleep and do more physical activity than most people, while constantly facing life and death situations and never quitting.

BUD/s, which stands for Basic Underwater Demolition/ SEAL training is the first phase of the Navy SEALs training course. This phase of the training has an attrition rate of 70-85%.[76] Trainees go through a notorious segment called Hell Week, in which they endure five days and nights of grueling training with only a couple hours of sleep. When asked what the key is to passing BUD/s, Navy SEAL, author, and entrepreneur Jocko Willink stated, "Just don't quit".[77]

Enduring the difficult trainings and eventual battle situations requires these soldiers to focus only on what's within their control in that moment. If they think about everything that'll be required of them in the hours, days, and months ahead, they'll most likely feel overwhelmed. When that happens, soldiers quit. To develop resilience and push through grueling situations without getting engulfed by stress, they must learn to direct their focus on the present and the task in front of them.

Your Inner Rival will always be there telling you it's too hard, until you decide, no matter what, you're not going to quit. That's the true definition of resilience.

People and Resilience

Resilient people face the same events and challenges in life that non-resilient people face. What sets them apart is the way they respond to those events and challenges. According to studies, people respond to stressful events in one of four different ways:

1. They become overwhelmed by the effort they need to put forth when taking on a challenge or situation. They are unable to adapt, learn, or give their best effort because they're emotionally drained.
2. Some become more aggressive. In trying to get the right response to an adverse situation, they become frightened at the outcome and respond with extreme emotion.

3. Others feel sorry for themselves thinking the situation is unfair. They feel as if they always get the short end of the stick. They play the victim role.

4. There are those who adapt with great resilience. They may not always win, but they persevere and grow.[78]

An athlete could use one of those four alternatives in response to getting cut from a team in tryouts:

1. After seeing that there are lots of good players at tryouts, the athlete decides it's not worth even trying because they wouldn't make it on the team anyway.

2. When they get cut, they get angry and say things like, "I didn't want to be on the team anyway." Or "The coach has no idea what they're doing."

3. They feel sorry for themselves and ask questions like, "Why does the coach hate me?" And "I'm never going to be good enough to make the team." They play the victim card.

4. The fourth athlete is resilient, and even though they don't make the team they approach it with a learning attitude. They ask the coach what they need to improve upon and then set goals and build a routine for how they are going to develop their game to make the team next year.

Everyone faced the same challenge, but not everyone approached it with the same attitude. Resilient people believe they have influence over the course of events in their lives. They look for positive meaning and purpose to things that happen. They believe they can learn from both negative and positive experiences.[79] If you don't see yourself fitting into the fourth category, you can learn to get there.

After graduating from college, I wanted to pursue my dream of being a college basketball coach. I didn't know that by choosing that profession, I would experience a healthy dose of humility and a big lesson in resilience.

Because I didn't play college basketball, people didn't put much stock in my knowledge and abilities to coach the game. I understood that. I was brand new to the profession. But the continued stigma burned on the inside. I didn't yet realize that I was going to have to fight and get turned down for multiple positions in order to move forward.

Coaching is an extremely competitive profession. Unless you're at the pinnacle, salary generally isn't the best. Many coaches work hard and deal with the daily grind for a small amount of money. I was no different. But that wasn't necessarily where my resilience was built. It grew from having to write hundreds of letters and emails, followed up with countless phone calls to coaches while trying to make connections and join coaching staffs. Once I even waited three hours for a newly hired head coach at a Buffalo Wild Wings while he gave a radio interview. He was kind enough to take my resumé and listen to me talk for five minutes. I never heard from him again.

Another time I interviewed with a head coach and athletic director from a school in the Midwest, who both thought I'd be great for the staff and wanted to hire me. I couldn't have been more excited to start with this university. As soon as I got out of the meeting, I called the coach I then worked for. That coach, Matt, is one of my best friends and mentor. I told him the exciting news. As he got done congratulating me, he told me he was just diagnosed with cancer. My world was rocked! I just told my mentor and best friend I was leaving his staff when he was about to go into the biggest battle of his life! But he made the conversation about me and not him.

I met with Matt and the team to let everyone know I would not be coming back next year. I had one last follow up meeting with the HR Director from that Midwestern university I was so excited to work for. Believe it or not, *she* decided I wasn't a good fit for their basketball program! I was devastated!

Again, I immediately reached out to Matt. He, his staff, and team welcomed me back with open arms and showed me the grace that I so desperately needed!

Through these experiences and more I began to understand that to achieve my goals, I had to get back up after getting knocked down over and over. I eventually made it on staffs at other universities, but it did take many more letters and phone calls to get there.

Change Your Perspective

The way you perceive stress, challenges, and threats is important to how you view and approach new situations. Seeing setbacks and challenges as opportunities to grow gives them unique value and meaning., This is the mindset of someone who is resilient.

If you view stress, setbacks, or challenges as bad things that "happen" to you, you will feel sorry for yourself instead of growing. That feeling invariably leads to self-loathing and quitting.

The setbacks often feel uncomfortable. But they can also be used as opportunities to strengthen yourself mentally, physically, or emotionally. When you view adversity as a way to grow and improve, it won't feel quite as defeating if things go wrong. By knowing in your heart that nothing great is ever achieved without setbacks and stumbles, you will be more likely to embrace challenges and have the drive to push forward through them.

Handling what I viewed as continued rejection was a big mental hurdle for me. I often felt sorry for myself and asked, "Why does this always happen to me? When will someone realize I'm a good basketball coach? What more do I need to do?" This internal monologue loop went on in my head for years. It started to send me to a place where I cared too much about what other people thought. I focused on things that were out of my control. I developed the anxiety that eventually took me out of coaching basketball.

My anxiety went to the next level when I let my anxiety and panic attacks win and quit basketball because of them. "Does that mean I'm a quitter and not resilient?" I wondered. Once I stepped away from coaching, I had to go through this battle with my Inner Rival daily. It didn't always end in my favor. My Inner Rival often got the best of me. I reached a low place where I didn't want to deal with anyone anymore. That is when I realized something needed to change.

When I changed my perspective, I realized I wasn't a quitter for not coaching basketball anymore. It actually took courage to look deep enough at myself to realize this was a necessary step for me to continue to develop as a person. I began to appreciate that there is more to life than worrying about what others think. As long as I am proud of my effort, that's good enough for me. That may not sound like much, but it can be difficult for many coaches to get to that point. They are often judged by others on every decision they make.

I have learned to get my mental health under control and find a better balance in my life. I've found a new calling in helping athletes, coaches, performers, and anyone else who wants to become mentally stronger. I've accepted the challenge of writing this book and building a business, which has given me plenty of opportunities to overcome new challenges and setbacks. I continue to push on!

The key for me was to stop beating myself up and acknowledge the courage it took for me to step away from something I had built my identity around. Ending one chapter doesn't mean I'm weak. It gave me the chance to start a new chapter with a new calling and new challenges. It all began to change when my perspective changed.

Resilience and the Brain

The brains of people who are resilient grow to look different from those who are not. In his book, *The Emotional Life of Your Brain*, Dr. Richard Davidson writes that the amount of activation in the left side prefrontal cortex region of the brain of a resilient person can be up to thirty times greater than in someone who is not resilient. Davidson also discovered that the quantity of signals that go back and forth from the prefrontal cortex to the amygdala determines how quickly the brain recovers from stress. Our brain's fight or flight response is located in the amygdala. The more activation the prefrontal cortex has, the shorter the time period the amygdala has being in control. In other words, the stronger your prefrontal cortex, the less time you'll have to deal with your body's fight or flight response and stress.

In later research Davidson used MRIs. He confirmed that people who were more resilient had more white matter (axons connecting neurons) lying between the prefrontal cortex and amygdala. This is because the prefrontal cortex is able to turn down the signals from the amygdala that is associated with negative emotions. In contrast, less resilient people had less white matter, therefore less ability to quiet those signals.[80]

The brain can be strengthened with effort over time like a muscle. One of the best ways to strengthen your prefrontal cortex, decrease the activation in your amygdala, and strengthen the connection between the two is through a method previously discussed - meditation! By meditating, you're taking a proactive approach to strengthen your resilience. It will prepare your brain to better deal with stress and adversity, thus allowing you rationally to take on challenges that at first may seem overwhelming.

Meditation has been one of the most effective ways to turn down the volume on my own Inner Rival and become more resilient. Difficult situations don't feel overwhelming, and I'm able to think more clearly about how I want to approach the challenge in front of me. I have improved my ability to embrace the rough times, as I know they'll make me a stronger person.

Something Went Wrong? Good!

American author, podcaster, and retired US Navy Officer Jocko Willink is known for many different things. One that has been beneficial to me is what I call the "Good Mindset".[81] In one of his early episodes of the *Jocko Podcast*, he said that every time one of his soldiers came to him with a problem, he responded "Good." When asked by the soldier why this was always his response, Jocko replied, "When things are going bad, there's going to be some good from it." Here are examples of how this mindset works:

- Didn't get the promotion? Good. Now you have more time to learn and prepare for the next opportunity.
- Raining outside while you're training? Good. You'll learn to work through harder conditions, and you won't get sweaty.
- Tore your ACL playing sports? Good. You get more time to train your upper body and work on your mental toughness.
- Your bike has a flat tire? Good. You have the chance to walk to work.

- Lost the game? Good. You have an opportunity to learn what you did wrong and how to improve.

The "Good Mindset" isn't meant to make things easier in life. It's meant to help you avoid self-pity when things go wrong and learn to see the value in any situation. Things often don't go according to plan. Your ability to be resilient can be determined by how you direct your focus and how you view the situation in front of you. The next time something goes wrong, don't get angry or frustrated. Try telling yourself, "Good. Here's an opportunity to figure out how to make it a positive experience."

Fixed Versus Growth Mindset

The fixed versus growth mindset is a concept that has garnered a great deal of attention over the last decade. Author and psychologist Carol Dweck has done years of research in this area and believes that there are two basic types of mindsets that people have. The *fixed mindset* means everything is the way it is. You have a finite level of ability and talent in everything you do. Whereas the *growth mindset* believes you can always improve and get better in any area you choose. You are never finished growing if you choose to work on it.[82]

A few examples of the fixed mindset versus growth mindset:

- Fixed: I'll never be good at math.
- Growth: I'm not very good yet, but if I keep studying, I'll get better.

- Fixed: John is a much better basketball player than I am.
- Growth: John is better at basketball right now, but I'll keep working on my skills and improve.
- Fixed: Why should I even try? She's going to win the race anyway.
- Growth: She is really fast! But I'm still going to try and keep up with her.

The fixed mindset looks at things in a way that's absolute. You're either good or you aren't. It avoids challenges and gives up easily. It often looks for excuses and ways to point the finger elsewhere when things don't go according to plan. The Inner Rival thrives on the fixed mindset.

With the growth mindset all those thoughts change and the Inner Rival quiets down. Rather than avoid challenges, someone with the growth mindset looks for ways to improve while taking on challenges. Someone with the growth mindset doesn't give up because they know there's something to learn no matter the outcome if they try their hardest. They understand they can be good at anything if they are willing to put in the time and effort.

As a tennis coach, I often saw the fixed mindset slow down the growth of many athletes. They often cared more about winning games in practice and looking good than learning to hit the shot with correct form. This was because it's more difficult to learn to hit the tennis ball correctly than it is to simply get it over the net. The players who got the ball over any way they could have had early success. But by not using good form on their strokes; they were setting themselves up to have less success in the future. Their ceiling for improvement was low.

I would see athletes who were taking the time to learn how to hit the ball correctly and be in the right position during points. They may not have had quite as much success early on because it can be difficult to learn to hit the ball correctly, but they had a much higher ceiling for improvement. As they stuck with it, their growth eventually came at a faster pace than someone with poor form.

The players who had the growth mindset usually played longer and improved more in our junior programs because they saw a steady pace of improvement over the years. The more time they put in, the better they became. The players who had the fixed mindset and saw early success eventually were passed in skill level by other players and often lost more games in the long run. Because they hadn't learned the basics in the beginning, they began to plateau in skill level sooner.

The fixed mindset cares a lot about what other people think and wants to win because it "looks good," whereas the growth mindset cares about improvement and understands success will come with persistence and as skills improve. The fixed mindset tends to be short-term thinking. The growth mindset pays more attention to what can be done now to be continuously successful in the future.

Grit

Grit is another area of study that has become popular in recent years. Angela Lee Duckworth, former teacher turned psychologist and author of the popular book *Grit,* defines grit as "passion and perseverance for very long-term goals." She writes: "Grit is having stamina. Grit is sticking with your future day in day out, not just for the week, not just for the month, but for years, and working really hard to make that future a reality. Grit is living life like it's a marathon not a sprint".[83]

Duckworth performed a study in a Chicago public school to see if there was a correlation between grit and the likelihood the students would graduate. She gave high school juniors a "grit questionnaire" and waited to see who graduated. She found that the students who were grittier were more likely to graduate. She believes the best way to build grit in kids is through the growth versus fixed-mindset model. Students learn and understand if they put in the effort over time, they can improve and become grittier.

Duckworth states, "having grit is the ability to stay persistent after a long-term goal."

A great example of this is Eric Butorac, my older brother. He graduated from Gustavus Adolphus College, a Division III school with a prestigious tennis program. When he graduated, he was planning on being a teacher. But for some crazy reason he had the idea to give his dream a chance and play professional tennis.

In the beginning of his pursuit, he had to move to France. He barely knew the language, drove all over the country playing tournaments, and practiced every day. He spent nights sleeping in his car or locker rooms or the occasional couch. He ate pasta with ketchup and mayonnaise for meals.

The tournaments felt especially difficult. He had only a small support system in France, consisting of just a couple of friends who were trying to achieve the same goals. He once lost a match in northern France in the morning, drove ten hours to southern France, and lost another match in the evening. He was knocked out of two tournaments on the same day! But he didn't give up. He stayed resilient.

One of the reasons he stayed so resilient was that he had the growth mindset. He understood if he continued to work on his craft, he would find ways to improve, and he did. He worked with different coaches, he asked questions and learned from players who came before him, found new ways to train his mind and body, and improved his nutrition. He took the losses he encountered and learned ways to make changes so the same mistakes didn't continually happen. He learned and he improved.

After years of hard work and sacrifice, he made it to the pinnacle of professional tennis, the ATP Tour. He was ranked as high as seventeenth in the world in doubles, made it to the finals of the Australian Open, and traveled the world playing tennis. None of it would have been possible without a passion for his goal and a strong showing of resilience, grit, and a growth mindset. He truly is the perfect example of the qualities working in unison.

Building a solid sense of resilience is a major step in quieting your Inner Rival. When you know deep down, you're not going to quit, no matter what, your Inner Rival isn't nearly as strong. It will still be there whispering in your ear *"you should quit."* But your resilient voice is louder and will drown out the Inner Rival. Promise yourself you'll never give up, and you'll be amazed at what you can achieve. Like Jocko said, "Just don't quit."

The following exercises will help you improve your resilience:

1. *Create goals you're passionate about.* When you're pursuing something, you truly believe in and want, you'll push through the tough times to be successful. If you aren't connected to the *"why it's important to you,"* then it will be difficult to power through the obstacles. Make sure you believe in your *why*.

2. *Meditate.* Meditation is a great way to strengthen your prefrontal cortex, which is crucial for regulating your fear and anxiety. Through daily meditation, you'll strengthen your ability to stay mindful and resilient when faced with adversity.

3. *Check your habits.* It is easier to be resilient when you physically feel well. If you are eating poorly, not getting enough sleep, or slacking on your exercise and movement, you will find it more difficult to be resilient when it is needed. Make sure that your daily habits are putting you in a position to feel your best.

Chapter 8
SELF-TALK

*"Be careful how you are talking to yourself
because you are always listening"*
—Lisa M. Hayes

The Inner Rival

Your Inner Rival is the voice filling your head with self-doubt, negativity, and constant chatter. It's the voice telling you that you can't reach your potential and you'll let everyone down if you even try. By taking control of the voice, you get to determine what it says and how it says it. Your self-talk can either be your biggest rival or your loudest cheerleader. You have the power to choose.

The Power of Self-Talk

Our minds never really stop thinking, whether we are conscious of it or not.[84] In fact, it's been said that we say roughly fifty thousand words to ourselves every day. That's the length of a novel. With so many words spoken aloud or in our thoughts daily, it's extremely important to make sure as many of those words are positive and productive as possible. For many of us, if left unchecked, our minds go in a negative, fearful, or skeptical direction.

The way you speak to yourself is vital to your success. This is true during practice, and before, during, and after competitions. In a meta-analysis of thirty-two different studies, it was shown that self-talk is effective in helping athletes. When used correctly, it improves performance and chances for success.[85] It also builds confidence, reduces fear and stress, improves focus, and helps to overcome doubt. This study also found that people who practice and persist in developing their self-talk would maximize their chances for the biggest improvement. But if used incorrectly, it can do the exact opposite. It will lower confidence, add fear and stress, reduce focus, and add new doubts. The importance of learning how to speak to yourself correctly cannot be emphasized enough.

The Negative of Self-Talk

Research has shown that up to about 77 percent of our thoughts are negative or counter-productive in some way.[86] It's no wonder we find it difficult to stop negative self-talk. Repetition is the key to mastery. If 77 percent of the fifty thousand words we say to ourselves each day is damaging, we're saying around 38,500 negative things to ourselves every day! The more we do it, the easier it becomes, and the spiral continues.

The left hemisphere of the brain's prefrontal cortex deals with challenges and rational thinking. It maintains an even balance emotionally and mentally. People who are more positive actually grow more neurons in that half of their prefrontal cortex. People who tend to be more negative grow more neurons in the right hemisphere of their prefrontal cortex. The right hemisphere is known for things such as pessimism, emotion, and imagery.[87] The more time you spend using either the left (positive) or right (negative) hemisphere of your brain, the more neurons you will grow in that area and the more dominant it will become.

The way you speak to yourself has a dramatic impact on your focus, motivation, confidence, resilience, and stress levels. It's important to become aware of *what* you're saying to yourself and noticing *when* it's negative. There can be many emotional highs and lows within one performance or game. Staying aware of your self-talk is a huge step in managing your physical, mental, and emotional arousal levels.

People negatively speak to themselves in several ways:

1. *Filtering – You pay attention only to the negative things that happened during a situation and filter out all the positives.* In a basketball game, you turn the ball over two times, and you think you had a terrible game. You filter out your fifteen points, five rebounds, and your team's victory.

2. *Personalizing – You take a situation and assume it's your fault.* The coach takes you out of the game for a quick rest. But you assume they take you out because you're not playing well.

3. *Catastrophizing – Something small happens and you automatically anticipate the worst.* You lose the first game of the tennis match,

and you assume you will play terribly the rest of the match.

4. *Polarizing – Things are either good or bad.* There isn't any in-between. You either play great or you play terribly.

It is important to become aware of the type of self-talk you are using when you want to get away from the negatives. People will often use more than one type of negative self-talk. It can be a good exercise to write down the negative phrases and words you use with yourself to see if there are any patterns. Once you are aware of what you say, you can begin to make the necessary changes.

I have used each one of these types of negative self-talk, especially during the build up to and height of my anxiety and panic attacks. In something as emotionally charged as athletics, it can be difficult not to negatively self-talk. My problems surfaced because I wasn't aware of the words, I was using with myself and the harm they were doing. I was just mindlessly being hard on myself. Once I began to understand what I was saying to myself and the situations in which I said it, I could begin to address it and make the needed changes.

I still catch myself being negative from time to time. I don't think that ever completely goes away for anyone. But the difference is I catch myself doing it almost immediately. I then try to correct myself into making it something positive and productive.

Five Levels of Self-Talk

In his book *What to Say When You Talk to Your Self*, Dr. Shad Helmstetter writes about the importance of the way you speak to yourself and the five different levels of self-talk that we use (I will not go into the fifth level of self-talk in this book as it is more of a spiritual type of self-talk. If you are interested, I recommend learning more about it.)

Level One – Negative Acceptance

This is the negative self-talk most of us encounter in our daily lives. You say something negative about yourself, and you immediately accept it as fact.

It includes phrases like:

"I can't."
"I won't be able to."
"I wish I could."
"I'm just too tired."
"I just can't seem to do it."

Your subconscious listens to everything you tell it and takes it as truth. If you tell yourself you can't, then you can't. Whether you're saying these words out loud or in your mind with words and images, you're programming your belief system to believe you're unable to be successful. Every time you say it, that belief gets stronger.

This type of self-talk can wreak havoc in your life. If you're incessantly pushing negative thoughts and images upon yourself, there's no telling how many amazing things you'll keep yourself from achieving. This type of thinking creates average achievers who do just enough to get by but not enough to achieve anything great. Negative talkers talk themselves into staying in their comfort zone. That's where you'll stay if you don't do the work to redirect negative self-talk.

Level Two – Recognition and Need to Change

Level two self-talk seems like it's in the right direction. You're recognizing the need to change. That's a good thing. But the fact that you're only *recognizing* the need to change and not actually changing might create even more negative self-talk. You're recognizing the need to change but not creating any type of positive solution to make the change.

This type of talk uses phrases such as:

"I should have…."
"I need to…."
"I really should go to the gym more often."
"I need to start eating healthier."
"I should get more batting practice."

If you were to continue those statements, they would end with "…but I'm not." That's why they are negative statements. Even though these seem like innocent statements, they end with the negative fact that you aren't doing something that you know you should. They create doubt, guilt, and disappointment in your own self-image. That's not a good thing.

Level Three – Decision to Change

This level of self-talk helps instead of hinders you. You are recognizing a need to change something. You're stating that you're making the change. This change is stated in the present tense, and it uses phrases like, "I never," or "I will no longer." With this type of self-talk, you're replacing the "can't" and "won't" with a new positive tone. You're telling your subconscious mind to make the change.

Suppose you want to get into better shape. You decide to stop eating sweets. You say to yourself, "I no longer eat sweets." You want to say this to yourself quietly as well as out loud. Every time you grab a sweet, say to yourself, "I no longer eat sweets," even if you do decide to eat it. Eventually you'll pick up that sweet and decide you don't want it. It doesn't appeal to you anymore.

What you're doing is reprogramming your subconscious to believe you no longer eat sweets. Your past programming, for whatever reason, was that you wanted sweets. It was programmed strongly into your subconscious. You need to reprogram your subconscious to no longer want them.

That takes time.

Level Four – The Better You

This is the most needed and powerful level of self-talk. It's also the least used by most people. This self-talk tells you that you can do whatever it is you set your mind to. The level four talker takes on challenges, doubts, fears, and problems in a productive way. He or she gets rid of the "cannots" and uses phrases like:

"I am..."
"I will..."
"I can..."

This level of self-talk programs your subconscious with positive thoughts and images. This programming improves your chance for success. It builds your confidence even in difficult situations and helps you rebound after a tough loss or bad performance. It not only finds the positive, it also guides you in the direction of improvement.

Become aware of the level of self-talk you're using. No need to judge yourself if you realize you're in level one or two. Just redirect your thinking into a positive and productive state and keep moving forward. The more often you do this, the more it will become a habit.

Performance Statement

Having the ability to stay in the moment and not let your thoughts carry you away is vital when trying to perform at your best. Extensive research in the field of sport psychology shows that an athlete's internal dialogue has a significant influence on their performance, whether it's positive or negative. One of the best ways to improve on this skill and stay focused in the moment is by creating a performance statement for yourself.

In his book, *10-Minute Toughness*, Jason Selk defines a performance statement as "a type of self-talk designed to help athletes zoom in on one specific thought to enhance performance consistency. It's a simple yet concrete thought that specifically identifies the process for success, or what it takes to perform at your best".[88]

Here are a few different examples of good performance statements for different sports:

- Tennis: "Watch the ball, follow through."
- Basketball: "High release, snap wrist."
- Baseball: "Track the ball."
- Golf: "Head down, eyes on the ball."

Follow these guidelines when creating one that works for you and your sport, performance, or situation.

1. *It should be short.* You want it to be something easy to remember and say to yourself quickly. It should not be a long-drawn-out statement. Just a few words are perfect. If it's too long and complicated, it will actually begin to distract you. You'll over-think what you are doing. Keep it simple!
2. *It should be positive.* Make sure it says what you *should* do, not what you *shouldn't* do. Your mind doesn't comprehend the negative words like can't, don't, and shouldn't. When you say things like "don't hit it in the net," your mind hears and sees "hit it in the net." Be positive, productive, and stay away from negative words.
3. *It should be actionable.* Make it something you can physically do.

Example of how to use a performance statement:
Charlie is a basketball player who is at the free throw line with the opportunity to win the game. He doesn't have a performance statement ready. During intense situations like this, it's easy to let in negative thoughts such as, "I really hope I don't miss this" or "If I miss this shot, I'll let everyone down." Charlie's mind pictures a missed shot. His body physically reacts as he becomes nervous. His heart rate increases, breaths shorten, and muscles tense up. All of this makes it much more difficult to make the shot.

Charlie needed a performance statement such as "eyes on the rim, high follow through." He would be focused more on the positive actions he wants to produce instead of the negative things that may stream through the mind. Our minds are not able to focus on two things at once. When we have a strong positive statement in place, the negative cannot burrow its way in.

Remember to phrase your statement in the positive. When you say to yourself, "don't miss this shot" or "don't brick it," your brain hears and sees "miss this shot" and "brick it." Your brain is unable to comprehend words like "can't" and "don't."

Don't think of a black cat.

What was the first thing you thought of? Most likely it was a black cat. We can't tell our minds *not* to do something. Instead of telling yourself "Don't miss this shot," use a positive and actionable statement such as "high follow through" or "high release, nothing but net."

Another benefit of having a good performance statement is its ability to bring you back into the moment. Daily meditation will aid in helping you notice when your mind is being carried away by negative thoughts or images. When this happens, you're not in the "moment" where you perform your best. Once you become aware of this, you can use your performance statement to focus back on the moment and be productive.

Identity Statement

Your identity statement is another extremely important type of self-talk to build into your routines and eventually turn into a habit. Unlike the performance statement, the identity statement isn't necessarily tied to a skill. It's related to an attitude and mindset. The performance statement is constructed to help you perform better in competition and raise your level of confidence in the moment by helping you focus on what's important. But the identity statement invokes more generalized positive emotions and characteristics that will put you in a place to perform your best.

There are two parts that go into your identity statement. The first part should be a positive characteristic you want to work on. The second part should be something you hope to accomplish or achieve.[89] It's okay if the second part is a bit of a stretch. But make sure it's somewhat realistic and achievable.

Examples of Identity Statements:
Hockey goalie: "I'm a brick wall; nothing gets past me."
Basketball point guard: "I'm calm; I make the right play."
Football running back: "I'm strong. I'm fast. I'm powerful."
Team: "We're never out of it; we always find a way to win."

Professional athletes use identity and performance statements all the time to help bolster themselves. One athlete who exemplifies this perfectly is Mohammad Ali and his identity statement: "I am the greatest!" He would say that over and over to himself and anyone who'd listen. He was continually telling his conscious and subconscious mind he was the greatest fighter alive and that no one could beat him. This helped give him the confidence to believe he was the best so he could perform at his best. He did all this even before he became the greatest in his sport.

Not only did Ali's identity statement become famous, so did his performance statement, "Float like a butterfly, sting like a bee." Through that performance statement, he was telling himself to stay light on his feet and powerful with his punches. He did it in a way that evoked strength both visually and emotionally. Ali understood the importance of owning the voice in his head and was a master at making it work to his advantage.

Tips for Continued Growth

Awareness Is Key

Make sure your self-talk is helpful. You need to be aware of what you're saying to yourself. Notice if there are events or times when you're more negative or when the inner chatter becomes too noisy. Once you're aware of the talk that's holding you back, then you can begin to change it. It can be more difficult to be honest with yourself than you'd think. Meditation is a great way to become aware of what you're saying to yourself. The more you meditate, the more you'll notice your inner dialogue.

A good exercise is to write down what words or phrases you often use with yourself. See if there are any patterns. Then you can change what you say to yourself if necessary.

Make It a Habit

As with your performance statement, you'll want to create your identity statement based on what works best for you. You will build it into a habit. If you try to use the statements only when you're in difficult situations, they won't do much good. As with any other skill, you need to practice using them. You would not try a new type of shot or pass in a game and expect to see success if you had never practiced it. The same goes for using the skill of positive self-talk. You must practice it constantly to see the enormous results it can bring.

Change It

When speaking to yourself, if you don't feel like it's having the impact you hoped it would, one option is to change the word "I" to the word "You." Research published in the *Journal of Personality and Social Psychology* claims that using "You" can be more effective than using "I" when speaking to yourself. Using the word "You" allows you to be more objective and use the feedback.[90] It's a small change, but sometimes a minor change can make all the difference in the world.

Ask for Help

Asking a trusted coach or teammate to help you brainstorm on performance and identity statements is a great way to start the process. Their outside perspective is invaluable. They may have some insights about you of which you weren't aware. Don't be afraid to ask for help. You don't have to do this alone.

Stay Vigilant

It can be easy to fall back into old habits. For most people, it's easier to be negative than it is to be positive. Make sure you're continually checking in with yourself to ensure you're feeding your brain positive words and images. It's worth the effort.

Be Your Biggest Cheerleader

If you're not kind to yourself, who will be? Being your biggest cheerleader doesn't mean telling yourself you can't do anything wrong or that you're perfect. It's more about holding yourself accountable and being truthful with yourself, while continuing to believe you can achieve your goals. It's about being honest about why you got knocked down and being the first to build yourself back up.

The type of self-talk you use will be your strongest ally or your biggest rival. If you make sure your self-talk is positive and productive, you will find it easier to overcome challenges and obstacles. But if you allow the Inner Rival to take over that voice, it will become negative. Those same challenges will seem too overwhelming and impossible. That's why it's important to stay vigilant, productive, positive, and powerful in your self-talk.

The following exercises will help you improve your self-talk:

Exercise 1

Changing Negative to Positive

Event	Negative Statement	Is there any real evidence or proof of this?	Positive statement change
Missed shot	"I can't make anything."	No, I've made shots before.	"Tough miss, Keep looking to score."
Dropped fly ball	"I stink at catching."	No, I play baseball at a high level.	"Just one drop, keep an eye on the ball."

Helpful Tip: When working on changing your self-talk from negative to positive, think about how you would speak to your best friend if they made a mistake. We're often harder on ourselves than on others. Think about how you'd try to help someone else focus. Work on using that with yourself.

Exercise 2

Creating a Performance Statement

Think of the best coach or athlete in your sport. Right before your big game, they give you advice. They tell you that if you focus on this one thing during the game, you'll succeed. What is that one thing? Take some time to think about it. If more than one thing comes to mind, that's fine. Write them all down. Think about them and see if one stands out for you. It's okay to have more than one performance statement for different situations, but make sure you don't have so many they become hard to remember and distracting. Most athletes stick with one or two statements. Here are a couple of examples:

Golf: "Head down, smooth and easy."
Softball: "See the ball, compact swing."

Now, you try a few:

1. _____
2. _____
3. _____
4. _____
5. _____

Use statements that are productive and free of negative words. They should state what you *want* to do, not what you *don't want* to do. They should clear unwanted chatter in your mind and help you stay focused on what you need to do to perform at your best.

Exercise 3

Creating an Identity Statement

Creating an identity statement is slightly different than creating a performance statement. Your identity statement should evoke some emotion or feeling in you. You want to identify with the qualities in this statement and honestly believe in them. What do you want to be? What attitude will help you perform at your best? When you figure that out, this statement will help you develop the qualities needed to achieve everything you want. It should be in two parts:

1. A strength or quality that you possess that sets you apart from the competition.
2. The positive outcome that you desire (it can be a stretch).

High Jump: "Strong legs, to soar like an eagle."
Football Lineman: "I'm a brick wall. I can't be moved."

Now, you try a few:

1. _____
2. _____
3. _____
4. _____
5. _____

Chapter 9

PREPARATION

*Life is all about preparation. Preparation
is all about hard work, sacrifice, discipline,
organization, consistency, practicing the right
concepts and more. I subscribe to the
wisdom of the oft-quoted sports maxim,
"The will to win is not nearly as important
as the will to prepare to win"*
—Harvey Mackay

The Inner Rival

Your Inner Rival likes to make being prepared seem as if it's not as important as it is. It will give you the sense that you've done enough to prepare and that your challenges ahead aren't as hard as they really are. It will make you feel overconfident while preparing. Then, just before you're about to compete, it will make you feel anxious and unsure about whether or not you're ready to take on the challenge ahead. This is a common trick that the Inner Rival likes to play right before an important event.

By mentally preparing for your competition, performance, event, or speech, you'll be ready for the obstacles ahead, whether you were expecting them or not. You'll stay calm in the face of adversity. You can respond with sound decision making instead of reacting emotionally to unexpected events. You'll be able to build a plan so you are confident knowing you've done everything you can to prepare. The only thing left to do is give your best effort.

Introduction

Even if you've done everything to prepare physically for a specific challenge ahead, you never know what curveballs might be thrown your way. If you haven't put in the time and energy to prepare yourself mentally as well, achieving success could become extremely difficult. Consistent mental preparation will give you the best opportunity to have consistent performances.

Adversity can come in all forms. Maybe you're a dancer and the lights go out during your performance. Or you're the back-up quarterback called to play in the second half of a big game after the starter gets injured. Or a baseball player who forgets your bat at home. Are you mentally ready to meet and overcome that adversity? By being mentally prepared for the unexpected, you'll be more likely to handle those troublesome scenarios successfully, rather than fold in the face of an abrupt challenge.

Not only does mental preparation get you ready to take on unforeseen tests, it also gets your mind and body prepared for the actions you *know* you'll need to take. It helps get your mind into a state of alertness best suited for what you're about to do. Whether you're a golfer, a rugby player, or pianist the tools you'll use to prepare are the same. But the ways in which you use them will be slightly different.

The world's top performers take the time to warm up both physically and mentally. This is true whether they're professional athletes, musicians, speakers, Special Forces Operators, or dancers. Physical and mental preparation go hand in hand. One does not supersede the other. Think of your physical and mental preparation as a cake with frosting. Your physical preparation is the cake. Your mental preparation is the icing on the cake. The mental preparation will make your physical preparation even better!

Benefits of Mental Preparation

Having the willpower and self-control to do the hard work necessary to be mentally prepared is not easy. In order to get the full benefit, preparation can't just be a sometimes thing. It needs to be an all the time thing. It takes discipline to get yourself into the right mindset before you perform and compete. But when you do it properly, the amount of success you will see can skyrocket!

Preparation is Helpful in Overcoming Adversity
When you plan for the possible scenarios you may encounter during your performance, your ability to overcome adversity increases. We know visualizing your performance is an important aspect of preparation. But you don't want to imagine everything only going right and having immense success. You'll also want to imagine all the different ways in which things could go wrong. Don't stop there. You must picture yourself overcoming those challenges and being

successful. You're preparing your conscious and sub-conscious for what to do when you find yourself in some unexpected circumstance. This almost always happens to some degree or another.

Preparation Boosts Confidence
Confidence going into an event is essential for peak performance. Your confidence level is a tricky thing that is influenced by many different factors. Confidence can come and go as quickly as the wind. Sometimes you don't know how to get it back. It's important to understand how to build and maintain it. Preparation is one method that will always help.

Preparation Helps to Motivate
By fully preparing, you can go into your performance with confidence. Because you are confident, you'll feel even more motivated to attack the challenges ahead. Because you are feeling motivated, any adversity you face will feel lessened and easier to conquer. You will know you've put in the time and energy to give your full effort in your performance. You won't want to waste that work by giving up. Your mental and physical plan is in place. All that's left to do is to execute.

Preparation Creates Self-Discipline
Self-discipline is critical to success in performance and life. It means pushing away the excuses and driving forward even if you don't feel particularly motivated. It means pushing away distractions to focus on what is important to you in your long-term

goals. By continuously preparing to do what is necessary for success, you will learn how to create a more self-disciplined life, which I personally believe also leads to a happier life.

**Preparation Can Help You Relax and Stay
*in the Moment***
When you're fully prepared with a plan, you are able to perform more freely. By not having to waste mental energy figuring out your plan on the fly, you'll feel calmer and in the moment during your competition. You will be able to execute your plan that is already in place and perform more focused and in the moment.

How To Mentally Prepare

Everyone has different personalities, emotions, fears, anxieties, and confidence levels. Everyone's needs are going to be slightly different when preparing for a competition or performance. But there are exercises *anyone* can do and *everyone* should do to help their mental preparation. Whether it's playing golf, competing in a wrestling match, or giving a speech, these mental exercises will help get you primed and ready to perform.

Days Before Performance
Your preparation for competition or an event doesn't just begin the day of or hours leading up to it. Depending on what the event is, your preparation should begin the days, weeks, or even months

preceding it. The more important the event, the more preparation time you'll want to have. Below are exercises you can do ahead of time to focus your mindset:

- *Visualize Success* – Visualize yourself being successful in different situations you might encounter. Do this a few times a day for at least a couple of minutes each time. When you get up in the morning and before you go to bed at night are two great times to practice this technique. Or find a quiet place where you can be alone, focus on your breathing, and become mindful. Use the visualization practice techniques I discussed in chapter three, or another visualizing technique you have learned, to see yourself performing at your best and overcoming challenges. This allows you to build your confidence and lower your anxiety in the days leading up to your performance. Do your best to make your visualizations as vivid and realistic as possible.

    As you go through your day, it is natural to have negative thoughts and images unexpectedly pop into your head about different things that could go wrong during your performance. Take action. Stop it immediately and replace it with an image of you being successful. This isn't always easy as our minds naturally go toward negative outcomes. But the more you practice seeing positive outcomes, the more natural and easier it will become for you.

- *Positive Talk* – Make sure the words you're saying to yourself in the days leading up to your event are preparing you mentally to perform at your best. Your Identity and Performance Statements are powerful tools to use at this time to help get you ready. Remember to use words and statements that are productive and constructive in helping you perform with confidence and poise.

A good way to see positive self-talk in action is when watching mixed martial arts fighters in pre-match press conferences and interviews. They're often very detailed and graphic when describing what they're going to do to their opponent. This isn't just for show or to intimidate the person across the octagon from them. It's to help create feelings of power, strength, confidence, and dominance in their own conscious and subconscious minds leading up to the fight. They are constantly bombarding themselves with strong, constructive self-talk. If they want to be successful in something as difficult as a cage match, there can be no room for self-doubt. The more you say it, the more your brain and body will believe it.

One phrase I often hear athletes and performers say in the days leading up to an event is, "I'm so nervous." This doesn't necessarily seem like a negative phrase, but every time you say it, you're reinforcing to the conscious and subconscious that you're unsure whether you will be able to handle your performance or competition. Instead of saying, "I'm nervous," change it to, "I'm excited." This may seem like a small difference, but when you're excited about something, you approach it with more assurance and conviction. But if you approach the same event experiencing nervousness, you'll feel more timid and less able to handle the challenges, real or imagined.

- *Create Your Plan* – Having a plan going into your event, performance, or competition is vital to your mental toughness. If you don't have a plan, your worry and anxiety will be heightened. You will be continuously reacting to events and trying to figure out what to do next. If you are focused on executing your plan, rather than distractions, it's easier to respond to adversity and get into the flow state or "the zone." That is where you'll perform at your best.

It's important for your mental toughness to have back up plans when things go wrong. Former Heavyweight Champion boxer Mike Tyson once said, "Everybody has a plan, until they get punched in the face." Meaning that it's easy to feel prepared until things go awry. By having back up plans for different scenarios, you'll be able to stay focused and switch gears if things do go wrong with Plan A.

The Special Forces in our military give us many good examples of this, one of which involves their mission preparation. When planning a mission, they go over every possible step from beginning to end and all things that could go right or wrong in between. They don't wait for problems to arise and then try to solve the problem on the fly. They create a plan for overcoming each potential problem or challenge that may come their way. Everyone knows exactly what their job will be and what will be expected of them in each scenario. By being prepared in this way, each soldier can focus on executing their job, rather than on the chaos that goes on around them during a mission. Once the plan is in place, they rehearse it as much as possible before it's time to put it into action.

Day of Performance

You're at the day of your competition. Where is your focus? It should be on executing the plan you already have in place for performing your best. If your mind is wandering and ruminating over all the things that could play out during your event, then you're losing precious focus and energy. The tools here are no different than the ones that you use preparing days in advance. This time it's more condensed.

You will want to go someplace where you can find roughly fifteen minutes of quiet time to practice the following tools. A good time to prepare for a competition is before you go out for pregame warmups. You don't want to feel rushed while doing them, so make sure you leave enough time to work. If you're preparing for a speech or performance that isn't necessarily a competition, the same ideas still apply. Take some time to go over what you're about to do both physically and mentally while you are alone. Focus on executing what you're about to do.

- *Become Mindful* – Take one to two minutes to focus only on your breathing. Pull yourself into the moment and clear your mind of all racing thoughts. Think of the example of setting the snow globe down in chapter 2. This will help you feel more in control. If you allow your emotions and worries to become overpowering and the moment to become too big, your chances of performing well drop dramatically. It can be difficult before a game or performance to do this, as arousal levels are generally higher before an important event. That's why we want to practice these tools until they become habits beforehand.

- *Visualize* – Once you feel calm and centered, take three to five minutes to picture previous times you were successful. Picture the past successes you've had and challenges you overcame. Remember how hard you worked and all the positive emotions of strength that came with it. Remind yourself that you earned this opportunity. If you believe this is your first chance to be successful, then project what you think it will be like having success with this new opportunity!

  For the next three to five minutes, picture yourself doing the activity you're about to do. Remember the tactics or plan you have going into your event. Picture yourself executing said plan to perfection. Imagine everything about it going right and your actions moving flawlessly. Picture yourself being successful and seeing yourself overcome any and all challenges to finish in triumph.

- *Self-Talk* – After you've taken the time to visualize, spend the next few minutes building yourself up verbally. Words of power, positivity, and strength can go a long way in building your confidence. Use your identity statement to get ready to perform. Make sure you've prepared your performance statements and are ready to use them when necessary. Your inner voice will become the coach that keeps you moving onward and upward, regardless of adversity.

- *Embrace your Feelings and Emotions* – You will no doubt have feelings of excitement or "pregame jitters," especially if the impending event is important to you. Don't try to run from or calm those feelings. Embrace the feelings of eagerness and anticipation and use that energy to your advantage. When harnessed and embraced, that excitement can be used to heighten your focus and awareness. Make sure you don't let those feelings become overwhelming. Stay mindful and positive.

  Top athletes and performers often use different types of media to achieve the emotional arousal levels best suited for them and the specific event. Music is a popular way for many athletes to get themselves "geared up" to compete. Do what works best for you. Music that "pumps you up" is what works for most athletes. But NBA player Russell Westbrook takes a different route. He prefers to listen to slow jams music before games. He already has a naturally high level of arousal. For him, achieving a sense of calm before the game generally creates a better performance.

While playing and coaching athletics, I feel I generally did a good job of getting to the right mindset going into competitions and practices. I was focused and ready to compete to the best of my ability. I had a game plan and knew what I wanted to do to execute it. But I wasn't mentally ready for the negative adversity that I might face.

If I would have done a better job of getting myself to a place of calm and productive thinking, then I most likely would have handled mistakes on the tennis court with more grace. Maybe I wouldn't have given the referees such a hard time as a basketball coach. By mentally preparing, I may have been more skilled at handling adversity and focusing effectively.

The following preparation exercises could be the difference between a hard lesson learned or an amazing performance:

Exercise 1

- *Create a Checklist.* Make a list of everything you need to be prepared for your event. What physical items do you need to bring? How do you want to mentally and emotionally prepare? What warm up exercises do you want to do? By making a list, you'll be less likely to forget something and have more peace of mind while performing.
- *Prepare Before You Are Rushed.* Take time to prepare well ahead of your actual need. When you're rushed, it's easy to be forgetful or easily flustered.
- *Avoid Distractions.* Practice staying focused on the task at hand throughout the days leading up to an event. It's not always possible to ignore *all* distractions, especially at events with lots of commotion. By working at strengthening your focus on a daily basis you will be prepared to do your best.

Chapter 10

REVIEWING PERFORMANCE

"The capacity to learn is a gift;
the ability to learn is a skill;
the willingness to learn is a choice"
—Brian Herbert

Inner Rival

If you lose a game, make a mistake, or flounder during a performance, your Inner Rival makes it easy for you to focus on all the negative things that happened. It highlights the mishaps, blunders, missteps, and bad decisions. It makes it more difficult to see the positive things you did and your successes along the way, whether big or small. Even if you win, your Inner Rival will try to replay the negative incidents that happened and slip-ups you made that can take away the joy of competing hard.

Your Inner Rival might also give you every excuse for being unsuccessful. It points the finger in every direction except yourself. It tells you it was never your mistake and the only reason you didn't win was because of *x, y,* and *z,* which are out of your control. Everything is the fault of someone or something else.

Your Inner Rival can be very tricky. When you win or have a great performance, your Inner Rival will make you forget to look at the areas you should work on. It may highlight only the things that went well and cause you to ignore all you could've learned from your performance. It makes you assume everything will go just as well next time, turning your humble confidence into cockiness.

By reviewing your performance objectively, you'll learn and grow every time you perform, whether it's practice or an important event. Observing your performance and processing feedback constructively and honestly is vital to improving your skills, building your confidence, and silencing your Inner Rival.

Introduction

After a performance, spend time reviewing everything that happened. This would be the equivalent of a coach and players watching game film, the military doing an after-action-review, or a performance review in the business world. You can learn and process what went well, what didn't, and build a plan for what you want to do moving forward. You'll be even more ready when the next competition or performance arrives.

As important as review is to growth and success, it's amazing to me how many people don't pay attention or respond to the feedback they receive from failures and victories. When working with athletes, it's apparent to me which ones pay attention to feedback and adjust accordingly. They are the ones constantly tweaking their performance skills, especially when learning something new. At times this means taking a step back in ability level to take two steps forward later. The players who don't pay attention to feedback and care only about immediate success often plateau early because they aren't making the necessary changes.

In this chapter, I'll explain why a performance review is valuable to your mental toughness and how to evaluate your mindset in relation to your performance. Understanding where your attention was when things did or didn't go well is essential for learning how to strengthen your mindset for the next time and silence your Inner Rival.

Keys To a Quality Performance Review

Honesty

Whether you're reviewing your actions or mindset, honesty is the most important attribute to a good review. It means being honest about the things that went well and the things that didn't go well. This can be a struggle for most people because they tend to pay attention to only either the positive or the negative. If you're not honest with yourself on both sides, your improvement will eventually stall out.

Being honest about what went wrong during your performance, and why, is a great way to improve physically and mentally. If you aren't trying to find areas you can improve or reasons why an error was made, chances are you'll make many of the same errors again and again. This will create frustration and anxiety. Mistakes can be a good thing, but only if you learn from them.

Honesty is also important when you do perform well. When something goes right, it's okay to feel good about your actions. When you focus only on the good and assume it will continue, you can face issues in the future. Figure out why you performed well, do your best to replicate it, but understand the same performance is not guaranteed next time.

It's okay to tell yourself, "Good job" when you do things correctly and have success. If you look only for errors, it will be easy to get down on yourself rather than being proud of what you've accomplished. This sounds obvious, but you'd be surprised how many people aren't honest with themselves when they have a good performance. They see only the mistakes they made or things they should have done differently. Be honest about what you did well and what you didn't. That's the quickest way to improvement.

Review Without Judgement

Now that you are being honest with yourself about your level of execution, be careful not to judge yourself based on the outcome. You are not your performance. This goes for both the positive and negative. If you had a bad recital, missed the last-second shot, or stumbled through your speech, it doesn't mean you're a bad or foolish person. It doesn't mean everyone dislikes you and thinks you're not worthwhile. It's easy to feel that way if you didn't accomplish your goals. It simply means that you didn't have a great performance—that's it!

I honestly believe the most important part of anything you do is your answer to the question, "Did I give it my best effort?" If your answer is yes, then no matter the outcome, the fact that you didn't quit on yourself, or your team is always commendable. It's nice to have the outcome go your way. But even if it doesn't, your honest belief that you put in your best effort is what matters most.

If things *do* go well, stay humble and don't become overconfident in your ability. Too often I see an athlete or team have a great performance in one game, then turn around and play subpar their next. The athletes now feel so good about themselves that they've become overconfident and don't take the time to prepare mentally or physically for the next competition.

The best way to review your previous performance is without judgement, which isn't always easy to do. The more important the situation felt to you, the harder it can be to detach from the emotion of it and review without judgement. You want to do your best to look at your actions and outcomes with an objective eye. If this is difficult, watch yourself the way you would watch another performer on TV. Most likely, you'd pay attention to their actions and not judge their character as a person. Once you remove the emotion, figure out the steps you need to take to improve for next time. This is easier said than done. But it will help you focus where it is productive, move forward constructively, and prevent your Inner Rival from taking control of your mental state.

Review Your Mindset

Reviewing your mindset and focus before and during the event is equally important as reviewing your actions. Your mind is the reason you take the actions you do. If you pay attention only to the actions, that's like treating only the symptoms of a disease. Take time after your performance to analyze where your attention was while preparing for the event, where your focus was when things went good or bad, and where your levels of arousal were during competition. This will undoubtedly improve your ability to get your head in the right space when it's most crucial.

Most people don't take the time to assess what went right or wrong mentally because it can be extremely difficult. There's no video tape you can watch. No one else could see what you were thinking. Your own personal biases and perspective affect your assessment. Objectivity without judgement is imperative. If you can be truthful with yourself about your focus during the critical moments, you will be better positioned to understand what you need to do to get mentally prepared and locked in. The more you work on this, the easier it will be to recall your past mindsets.

Moving Forward

You have now reviewed your previous performance and made notes on what went well and what you need to improve. You've also assessed your mindset throughout your preparation and during your event. The next step is to map out what you can do to better position yourself mentally for your next performance. Reviewing your previous outcome is great, but if you don't have a plan to make the necessary improvements, you're more likely to make the same or similar mistakes again.

As a coach and athlete, I've spent many hours reviewing tapes and mapping out ways to improve and move forward. But one thing I had never done, though I wish I had, was to figure out where my mindset and focus was as a player during critical points of the game or match. I was so negative with myself, especially on the tennis court. It would've been a fantastic learning experience for me to figure out when my thoughts went negative and practice turning those around. If I had done so, I would have been able to make a conscious effort to stay mentally stronger and combat the Inner Rival were it to arise. But because I didn't review where my mindset was, I wasn't able to take any of these steps to improve that part of my game.

Even though the post-performance review can feel uncomfortable, it's a tremendously effective tool. Don't allow yourself to miss this opportunity. The benefits you receive mentally and physically from a good review and plan to improve are countless. Remember... Getting outside of your comfort zone and doing things that feel uncomfortable quiets the Inner Rival.

The following exercises will help you review your performance:

Exercise 1

Post-Performance Check In

- Fill this out after competitions. Doing so will provide you a brief level of understanding of both your performance and thought process.
- This will help to show you what your strengths and weaknesses were during your competition.
- There are no right or wrong answers.

Positive Performance Level of Performance Negative Performance

Played well	5 4 3 2 1	Played poorly
Felt excited	5 4 3 2 1	Felt anxious
Felt confident	5 4 3 2 1	Felt hesitant
I was resilient	5 4 3 2 1	Gave up
Muscles were relaxed	5 4 3 2 1	Muscles were tight
Focused on the controllable	5 4 3 2 1	Focused on the uncontrollable
Felt focused	5 4 3 2 1	Felt distracted
Full Effort	5 4 3 2 1	Could have given more
High energy	5 4 3 2 1	Lacked energy

What were some of the thoughts running through your head during your competition?

Exercise 2

Ask yourself these questions to begin thinking deeper about your performance, including what you can learn from it and steps you can take to improve moving forward.

- What went well?
  - Were they things I could control?
  - Where was my mindset at that time?
- What didn't go well?
  - Were they things I couldn't control?
  - Where was my mindset at that time?
- Was I physically prepared going into the event?
  - Is there anything I can change to be more prepared physically?
- Was I mentally prepared going into the event?
  - Is there anything I can change to be more prepared mentally?
- Is there anything I should eliminate to have a better performance next time?
- What do I need to spend more time practicing having a better future performance?
- What is my plan moving forward?

Chapter 11
CLOSINGS

"The most important thing is to try and inspire people so they can be great in whatever they want to do."
—Kobe Bryant

The late Kobe Bryant has become a major inspiration for me over the years. Quite possibly even more so once he stepped away from the game of basketball. His mindset for new challenges, the smallest details, learning more, never quitting, and helping other people to reach their greatness is something I think about often. The quote from the beginning of this chapter hangs on the wall behind my desk. It reminds me that if I want to reach my goals, I need to put in a massive effort. It also reminds me of my purpose right now: to help others reach their potential.

My sincerest hope in writing this book and sharing my story is that you'll gain the tools and knowledge to keep pushing beyond whatever obstacles you face to achieve your greatness. Silencing your Inner Rival is a daily challenge and requires a physical, mental, and emotional effort. It's not something you will do once, twice, or even three times and master. It will be a journey of work throughout your life. If you choose not to work to silence it, you're essentially choosing to let it take over your life and make your decisions for you.

When I was in college, my grandpa gave me a list of ten life lessons that were important to him. I've included them at the end of this chapter. While writing this book, I began to think about what life lessons I would impart today if I were to write a list for my future grandchildren. I settled on two lessons I believe are game changers for attitude and mental toughness. These lessons, when taken to heart, will help silence your Inner Rival.

1. *Life isn't fair.* "That's not fair," is my least favorite sentence of all time, and I hear it often. I hear it from parents saying it to their kids, athletes who have a bad bounce, adults at work, and just about any other situation you can imagine in life. Here's the absolute truth. Life *isn't* fair. It never was, never is, and never will be. If anyone told you otherwise, I'm sorry, but they were lying.

   Have you ever noticed people tend to only say "life's not fair," when it goes against them? If the call goes against their team, or they catch a bad break, then life isn't fair. But if it does go their way or the lucky break happens *for* them, then it was deserved for some reason.

   I used to be a "that's not fair" kind of guy, too. And it wasn't that long ago. But one day, the realization that it's not fair hit me like a ton of bricks. That's when my perspective on so many things in my life changed. I realized I needed to shift my focus to what's within my control. I still may feel disappointment if something doesn't work out, but now it doesn't create the anxiety within me it once did. I no longer dwell on things that didn't go my way. I learn from the experience, control what I can, and keep moving forward. This allows me to take the reins on the situation and quiet my Inner Rival, rather than give it the opportunity to get louder with negativity and envy.

2. *Expect Adversity.* If you have expectations that everything will go smoothly, just the way you planned, chances are you'll often face frustration and disappointment. Rarely does *everything* go smoothly. The secret sauce to life is the ability to create a plan, do your best to execute it, work through adversity along the way, and readjust. The people who become champions and achieve incredible heights are the ones who learn to be the best at taking challenges head on and figuring out how to thrive within that adversity.

Both of these lessons created a new sense of calm within me the more I realized how true they really were. Of course, there will be adversity. The fact that life isn't fair is one of the things that keeps it interesting. You never know what good fortunes could come your way! (Notice how I used the tool of perspective to look at life not being fair as a way of good things happening instead of the negative perspective?) But unfortunately, most people don't see it that way. But if you're reading this book, you can start right now!

Silencing your Inner Rival isn't just for when you're feeling anxious or getting ready to compete or perform in an important event. It's a lifestyle. It's a habit. It's an everyday thing. To get the most out of life and not let your mind create barriers like stress, pressure, and fear, you must battle your Inner Rival every day. And just when you think you don't need to worry about it anymore, it will rear its ugly head and try to create new doubts within you all over again. The tools provided throughout this book will give you the power to maintain a strong mindset and combat negative thoughts and images.

There is no final destination or end game. You won't wake up one day having completely defeated your Inner Rival. It's a continual process of learning and growth. It's about enjoying the journey. It's about doing your best to develop the right mentality for a fun and fulfilling experience. Rather than limiting what you can achieve, be your biggest cheerleader. Push yourself harder than you thought possible. Get back up if you get knocked down. You can do it. You just have to convince that voice in your head!

Remember, the wolf that wins is the wolf you feed.

Grandpa Butorac's Ten Rules to Live By

1. Always be a good sport. When you win, say little. When you lose, say less.
2. Always do your schoolwork. You don't want to be known as a dumb jock.
3. Never use profane language, as this shows ignorance.
4. If you don't have anything good to say about your teammates, then don't say anything at all.
5. Eagles soar and ducks quack. Be an eagle.
6. Always remember your roots, as these are the friends who care about you the most.
7. When the going gets tough, the tough get going.
8. When you get down and out, remember the sun will always rise in the morning.
9. You can't win every game or match, but when you lose a game and you did your best, you didn't lose – you just ran out of time.
10. Always be a leader and not a follower.

ENDNOTES

Introduction
1. Samuels, 2016

Chapter 1
2. Moran, 2012
3. Martins, 1987
4. Archer, 2013
5. Cohen, 2016
6. Murphy, 2018
7. Afremow, 2013
8. Cohen, 2016

Chapter 2
9. Mumford, 2016
10. Feloni, 2017
11. Malcolm, 2012
12. Booth, 2017
13. Afremow, 2013
14. Cover Media, 2020
15. Athlete Equanimity, 2019
16. Moran, 2012
17. Kjolhede, 2012
18. Athlete Equanimity, 2019
19. Thompson, 2022
20. Walton, 2015
21. Ireland, 2014

22. Troncale, 2014
23. Walton, 2015
24. Basso, 2019
25. Athlete Equanimity, 2019
26. Divine, 2014
27. Dowling, 2014
28. Pierre Philippot, 2002

Chapter 3

29. Collier, 2021
30. Lindsay Ross-Stewart, 2014
31. MacKenzie, 2015
32. Smith, 2018
33. Mosher, 2014
34. Hanshaw, 2016
35. Cicio, n.d.
36. Garcia-Rill, 2008
37. Rollins, n.d.
38. Garza, 2019
39. Garza, 2019
40. Mousavi, 2011
41. Martens, 1987

Chapter 4

42. Hughes, 2014
43. Morin, 2020
44. Hendrickson, 2019
45. Hendrickson, 2019
46. Ryan, 2022
47. Zheng Cao, 2011

48. McMahan, 2017
49. Ebner, 2021

Chapter 5

50. Athletics, 2022
51. Roosevelt, 1910
52. Alan Henry, 2019
53. Cohen, 2016
54. Alan Henry, 2019
55. Page, 2020
56. Johnson, 2021
57. Stillman, 2018
58. Economy, 2019
59. Gleason, 2020
60. Reddit, 2019
61. Poirier-Leroy, 2021
62. The Mind of Kobe Bryant-My Workouts, 2019
63. K. Anders Ericsson, 2007

Chapter 6

64. Introduction to Perception, n.d.
65. Estrada, 2020
66. Lazarus & Folkman, 1984
67. Warren, 2019
68. Warren, 2019
69. Warren, 2019
70. Dhabhar, 2018
71. Patterson, 2022
72. Patterson, 2022
73. Dhabhar, 2018

74. Crum, 2017
75. Ladouceur, n.d.

Chapter 7

76. Atlamazoglou, 2021
77. Real, 2019
78. Bejan & Tontia, 2013
79. Bejan & Tontia, 2013
80. Hampton, 2019
81. Podcast, 2016
82. Dweck, 2006
83. Duckworth, 2013

Chapter 8

84. Spalakoglu, 2019
85. Antonis Hatzigeorgiadis, 2011
86. Helmstetter, 2017
87. Helmstetter, 2017
88. Selk, 2009
89. Selk, 2009
90. Ethan Kross, 2014

BIBLIOGRAPHY

Introduction

Dalton, K. (2020, April 17). *The Yips and How It Affected Numerous Baseball Careers*. Retrieved from Sportscasting: https://www.sportscasting.com/the-yips-and-how-it-affected-numerous-baseball-careers/

Samuels, D. (2016, September 13). *Who is Freddy P. Soft? Jim Harbaugh explains he's the voice responsible for soft players*. Retrieved from Football Scoop: https://footballscoop.com/news/freddy-p-soft-jim-harbaugh-explains-hes-voice-responsible-soft-players

Chapter 1: Goal Setting

Afremow, D. J. (2013). *The Champion's Mind: How Great Athletes Think, Train, and Thrive*. New York: Rodale.

Archer, T. (2013, January 8). *Jason Garrett trying to follow Nick Saban's process*. Retrieved from ESPN: https://www.espn.com/blog/dallas-cowboys/post/_/id/4704461/jason-garrett-trying-to-follow-nick-sabans-process

Cohen, R. (2016). *Sport Psychology: The Basics, Optimizing Human Performance*. London: Bloomsbury.

Jordan, M. (2000). *The National Research Center on Gifted and Talented (1990-2013)*. Retrieved from University of Connecticut: https://nrcgt.uconn.edu/underachievement_study/self-efficacy/se_section8/

Locke, E. A. (1968). Toward a theory of task motivation and incentives.

Organizational Behavior and Human Performance, 157-189.

Martens, R. (1987). *Coaches Guide to Sport Psychology*. Champaign: Human Kinetics Publishers, Inc.

Mathers, C. (2020, February 12). *A Goal without a Plan is Just a Wish: 3 Lessons for This Quote*. Retrieved from

Developing Good Habits: https://www.developgoodhabits.
com/goal-without-plan/

Moran, A. P. (2012). *Sport and Exercise Psychology: A Critical Introduction, Second Edition.* New York: Psychology Press.

Murphy, M. (2018, April 15). *Neuroscience Explains Why You Need To Write Down Your Goals If You Actually Want To Achieve Them.* Retrieved from Forbes: https://www.forbes.com/sites/markmurphy/2018/04/15/neuroscience-explains-why-you-need-to-write-down-your-goals-if-you-actually-want-to-achieve-them/?sh=5b939a757905

Parren, A. (2021, February 12). *Research Shows 43 Percent of People Expect to Give Up Their New Year's Resolutions by February.* Retrieved from www.Sundried.com: https://www.sundried.com/blogs/training/research-shows-43-of-people-expect-to-give-up-their-new-year-s-resolutions-by-february

Chapter 2: Mindful Meditation & Focused Breathing

Afremow, J. (2013). *The Champion's Mind; How great athletes think, train, and thrive.* New York: Rodale.

Athlete Equanimity. (2019, December 19). *Benefits of Meditation for Athletes.* Retrieved from YouTube: https://www.youtube.com/watch?v=66IKLnh8qXI

Julia C. Basso, A. M. (2019). Brief, daily meditation enhances attention, memory, mood, and emotional regulation in non-experienced meditators. *Behavioral Brain Research*, 208-220.

Booth, R. (2017, October 22). *Master of Mindfulness, Jon Kabat-Zinn: "People are losing their minds. That is what we need to wake up to."* Retrieved from The Guardian: https://www.theguardian.com/lifeandstyle/2017/oct/22/mindfulness-jon-kabat-zinn-depression-trump-grenfell

Cover Media. (2020, July 20). *New study reveals just how many thoughts we have each day.* Retrieved from Newshub.: https://www.newshub.co.nz/home/lifestyle/2020/07/new-study-reveals-just-how-many-thoughts-we-have-each-day.html

Bibliography

Divine, M. (2014). *Unbeatable Mind; Forge Resiliency and Mental Toughness to Succeed at an Elite Level.* CreateSpace Independent Publishing Platform.

Dowling, C. (2014, Summer). *The Breath of Feeling: How our Breathing Affects our Emotions.* Retrieved from Irish Association of Humanistic and Integrative Psychotherapy: https://iahip.org/page-1075650

Feloni, R. (2017, November 23). *After Interviewing 140Ppeople at the Top of their Fields, Tim Ferriss Realized Almost all of Them Share the Same Habit.* Retrieved from Business Insider: https://www.businessinsider.com/tim-ferriss-meditation-mindfulness-2017-11

Frankl, V. (2006). *Man's Search for Meaning.* Boston: Beacon Press.

Ireland, T. (2014, June 12). *What Does Mindfulness Meditation Do to Your Brain?* Retrieved from Scientific American: https://blogs.scientificamerican.com/guest-blog/what-does-mindfulness-meditation-do-to-your-brain/

Kjolhede, B. (2013, September 10). *Meditation: Change Your Mind, Change Your Life.* Retrieved from YouTube: https://www.youtube.com/watch?v=upNONoxskiw

Malcolm, I. S. (2012, February 22). *The Benefits of Mindfulness Meditation: Changes in Emotional States of Depression, Anxiety, and Stress.* Retrieved from Cambridge University Press: https://www.cambridge.org/core/journals/behaviour-change/article/abs/benefits-of-mindfulness-meditation-changes-in-emotional-states-of-depression-anxiety-and-stress/16CEFE3661C9173067A32827CE8F6010

Mani, M. (2018, August 10). *4 Ways How Meditation Changes Your Prefrontal Cortex (And How It Benefits You).* Retrieved from Outofstress: https://www.outofstress.com/meditation-prefrontal-cortex/

Moran, A. P. (2012). *Sport and Exercise Psychology.* New York: Psypress.

Mumford, G. (2016). *The Mindful Athlete; Secrets to Pure Performance.* Berkeley: Parallax Press.

Pierre Philippot, G. C. (2002). Respiratory Feedback in the Generation of Emotion. *Cognition and Emotion*, 605-627.

Thompson, J. (2022, January 7). *NFL Hall of Famer Troy Aikman says Aaron Rodgers is evidence that meditation makes better leaders.* Retrieved from Insider: https://www.insider.com/troy-aikman-meditation-makes-good-leaders-like-aaron-rodgers-2022-1

Troncale, J. (2014, April 22). *Your Lizard Brain.* Retrieved from Psychology Today: https://www.psychologytoday.com/us/blog/where-addiction-meets-your-brain/201404/your-lizard-brain

Walton, A. G. (2015, February 9). *7 Ways Meditation Can Actually Change The Brain.* Retrieved from Forbes: https://www.forbes.com/sites/alicegwalton/2015/02/09/7-ways-meditation-can-actually-change-the-brain/?sh=4a10e98a1465

Chapter 3: Visualization

Cicio, P. (n.d.). *Power of visualization.* Retrieved from Success Thinc: https://www.philcicio.com/power-of-visualization/

Collier, B. (2021, December 4). *A Soldier and a Visionary.* Retrieved from Pressreader.com: https://www.pressreader.com/usa/the-pilot-news/20211204/281590948850910

Garcia-Rill, E. (2008, November 5). *Reticular Activating System: Encyclopedia of Neuroscience.* Retrieved from Science Direct: https://www.sciencedirect.com/science/article/pii/B9780080450469017678

Garza, A. (2019, March 15). *How to Visualize like a Pro.* Retrieved from YouTube: https://www.youtube.com/watch?v=KucsxWerkNI&list=WL&index=14&t=3s

Garza, A. (2019, February 3). *Scientific Benefits of Visualization for Athletes.* Retrieved from YouTube: https://www.youtube.com/watch?v=VHISQ6xIGZE

Hanshaw, G. O. (2016). Effect of self-talk and imagery on the response time of trained martial artists. *Sport, Exercise, and Performance Psychology,* 259-265.

Lindsay Ross-Stewart, S. E. (2014). Characteristics Affecting How College Basketball Coaches Advised Their Athletes to Use Imagery. *International Journal of Coaching Science,* 02-23.

Bibliography

MacKenzie, D. (2015, January 10). *Visualization: The Most Powerful Thing in Golf*. Retrieved from Golf State of Mind: https://golfstateofmind.com/powerful-visualization-golf/

Martens, R. (1987). *Coaches Guide to Sport Psychology*. Champaign: Human Kinetics Publishers, Inc.

Mosher, C. (2014, December 23). *How to grow stronger without lifting weights*. Retrieved from Scientific American: https://www.scientificamerican.com/article/how-to-grow-stronger-without-lifting-weights/

Mousavi SH, M. A. (2011). The effect of mental imagery upon the reaction of athletes' anxiety during sport performance. *International Journal of Academic Research in Business and Social Sciences*, 342-345. Retrieved from Physiopedia: https://www.physio-pedia.com/Mental_Imagery

Rollins, S. (n.d.). *The power of visualization: improve your skill by training your mind*. Retrieved from EsportsHealthcare: https://esportshealthcare.com/power-of-visualization/

Smith, D. (2018, October 24). *Power of the mind 1: The science of visualization*. Retrieved from Science Abbey: https://www.scienceabbey.com/2018/10/24/power-of-the-mind-the-science-of-visualization-1/

Chapter 4: Control the Controllables

Ebner, N. (2021). *Finish Strong: A Father's Code and a Son's Path*. New York: Penguin Press.

Hendrickson, E. (2019, August 26). *How To Stop Worrying*. Retrieved from Scientific American: https://www.scientificamerican.com/article/how-to-stop-worrying/

Holiday, R. (n.d.). *Meditations by Marcus Aurelius: Book Summary, Key Lessons and Best Quotes*. Retrieved from Daily Stoic: https://dailystoic.com/meditations-marcus-aurelius/

Hughes, D. (2014, November 29). *How to think like Sir Alex Ferguson: The Business of Winning and Managing Success*. Aurum. Retrieved from Converge: https://www.converge.today/article/controlling-the-controllables

McMahan, I. (2017, November 22). *Hacking the free throw: the science behind the most practiced shot in sports.* Retrieved from The Guardian: https://www.theguardian.com/sport/2017/nov/22/free-throws-foul-shots-science-of-sports

Morin, A. (2020, May 11). *2 Psychological Tricks That Will Help You Stop Worrying About Things You Can't Control.* Retrieved from Forbes: https://www.forbes.com/sites/amymorin/2020/05/11/2-psychological-tricks-that-will-help-you-stop-worrying-about-things-you-cant-control/?sh=3d6d6c1737e6

Ryan, S. (2022, June 6). *Rob O'Neill - SEAL Team Six/ DEVGRU Operator The Man Who Killed Bin Laden | SRS #027.* Retrieved from YouTube: https://www.youtube.com/watch?v=Vm0fAae8x7Q&t=11453s

Zheng Cao, J. P. (2011). Performance Under Pressure in the NBA. *Journal of Sports Economics*, 231-252.

Chapter 5: Get Out of Your Comfort Zone

Alan Henry, R. F. (2019, September 26). *The Science of Breaking Out of Your Comfort Zone (and Why You Should).* Retrieved from Lifehacker: https://lifehacker.com/the-science-of-breaking-out-of-your-comfort-zone-and-w-656426705

Athletics, W. (2022, November 20). *One Mile Men.* Retrieved from World Athletics: https://www.worldathletics.org/records/all-time-toplists/middle-long/one-mile/outdoor/men/senior

Cohen, R. (2016). *Sport Psychology: The Basics.* London: Bloomsbury.

Economy, B. (2019, April 23). *Use the 40 Percent Rule to Break Trhough Every Obstacle and Achieve.* Retrieved from Inc.: https://www.inc.com/peter-economy/use-40-percent-rule-to-achieve-impossible.html

Gleeson, B. (2020). *Embrace the Suck.* New York: Hachette Books.

Johnson, B. (2021). *Exiting the Cast of Our Comfort Zones.* Retrieved from Optimize: https://www.optimize.me/plus-one/exiting-the-cast-of-our-comfort-zones/

Bibliography

K. Anders Ericsson, M. J. (2007, July). *The Making of an Expert*. Retrieved from Harvard Business Review: https://hbr.org/2007/07/the-making-of-an-expert

Page, O. (2020, November 20). *How to Leave Your Comfort Zone and Enter Your 'Growth Zone'*. Retrieved from Positive Psychology: https://positivepsychology.com/comfort-zone/

Patterson, E. (2022, September 5). *Stress Facts and Statistics*. Retrieved from The Recovery Village: https://www.therecoveryvillage.com/mental-health/stress/stress-statistics/

Poirier-Leroy, O. (2021, June 4). *Bob Bowman on Mental Toughness, Dreaming Big, and Performing Under Pressure: "The Golden Rules" Book Review*. Retrieved from Your Swim Book: https://www.yourswimlog.com/bob-bowman-mental-toughness-the-golden-rules-book-review/

Reddit. (2019, August 23). *An old post from a Team USA Trainer Rob on Reddit about Kobe's work ethic 6 years ago*. Retrieved from Reddit: https://www.reddit.com/r/nba/comments/cy27ky/an_old_post_from_a_team_usa_trainer_rob_on_reddit/

Roosevelt, T. (1910, April 23). *The Man in the Arena*. Retrieved from Theodre Rooselvelt Center: https://www.theodorerooseveltcenter.org/Learn-About-TR/TR-Encyclopedia/Culture-and-Society/Man-in-the-Arena.aspx

Stillman, J. (2018, August 14). *Science Has Just Confirmed That If You're Not Outside Your Comfort Zone, You're Not Learning*. Retrieved from inc: https://www.inc.com/jessica-stillman/want-to-learn-faster-make-your-life-more-unpredictable.html

The Mind Of Kobe Bryant - My Workouts (2019, September 12). Retrieved from YouTube: https://www.youtube.com/watch?v=3EHdbuisJzY

Chapter 6: Perception

Crum, A. J. (2017). The role of stress mindset in shaping cognitive, emotional, and physiological responses to challenging and threatening stress. *Anxiety, Stress, & Coping*.

Dhabhar, F. S. (2018). The Short-Term Stress Response – Mother Nature's Mechanism for Enhancing Protection and Performance Under Conditions of Threat, Challenge, and Opportunity. *Frontiers in Neuroendocrinology*, 175-192. Retrieved from https://www.ncbi.nlm.nih.gov/pmc/articles/PMC5964013/

Embody. (2021, April 13). *Good, Bad, We Shall See*. Retrieved from Embody: https://www.feelbetterdogood.org/this-week/good-bad-we-shall-see

Estrada, J. (2020, February 7). *How Your Perception Is Your Reality, According to Psychologists*. Retrieved from Well and Good: https://www.wellandgood.com/perception-is-reality/

Gordon, R. (2018, November 30). *Stress & The Power of Perception*. Retrieved from Humble Warrior Therapy: https://www.humblewarriortherapy.com/blog/stress-the-power-of-perception

Introduction to Perception. (n.d.). Retrieved from Lumen Learning: https://courses.lumenlearning.com/boundless-psychology/chapter/introduction-to-perception/

Ladouceur, P. (n.d.). *What We Fear More Than Death*. Retrieved from Mentalhelp: https://www.mentalhelp.net/blogs/what-we-fear-more-than-death/

Lazarus, R. S., & Folkman, S. (1984). *Stress, Apraisal, and Coping*. New York: Springer Publishing Company.

Patterson, E. (2022, September 05). *Stress Facts and Statistics*. Retrieved from The Recovery Village: https://www.therecoveryvillage.com/mental-health/stress/related/stress-statistics/

Warren, S. (2019, December 4). *Good vs. Bad Stress: The Critical Difference Between Challenge and Threat*. Retrieved from Somatic Movement Center: https://somaticmovementcenter.com/challenge-threat-stress-response/

Chapter 7: Resilience

Atlamazoglou, S. (2021, January 21). *How the Navy's 'Hell Week' reveals who has what it takes to be a SEAL*. Retrieved from NavySeals.com: https://navyseals.com/5436/how-the-navys-hell-week-reveals-who-has-what-it-takes-to-be-a-seal/

Bibliography

Bejan, R., & Tontia, f. (2013). The role of resilience in coping with stress in sports. *Procedia – Social and Behavioral Sciences*, 402-407.

Duckworth, A. L. (2013, May 9). *Grit: the power of passion and perseverance*. Retrieved from YouTube: https://www.youtube.com/watch?v=H14bBuluwB8

Dweck, C. (2006). *Mindset: The New Psychology of Success*. New York: Ballantine Books.

Green, R. (2014, December 24). *Louis Zamperini: The Story of a True American Hero*. Retrieved from The Unwritten Record: https://unwritten-record.blogs.archives.gov/2014/12/24/louis-zamperini-the-story-of-a-true-american-hero/

Hampton, D. (2019, November 10). *12 Strategies for Building Resilience*. Retrieved from The Best Brain Possible: https://thebestbrainpossible.com/resilience-mental-health-emotions/

Podcast, J. (2016, January 25). *Jocko Motivation "GOOD" (From Jocko Podcast)*. Retrieved from YouTube: https://www.youtube.com/watch?v=IdTMDpizis8

Real, L. (2019, February 13). *WHY YOU SHOULD NEVER QUIT – JOCKO WILLINK | London Real*. Retrieved from YouTube: https://www.youtube.com/watch?v=e7oxOAlFmzI

Chapter 8: Self-Talk

Antonis Hatzigeorgiadis, N. Z. (2011). Self-Talk and Sports Performance: A Meta-Analysis. *Association for Psychological Science*, 348-356.

Ethan Kross, E. B.-S. (2014). Self-talk as a regulatory mechanism: how you do it matters. *Journal of Personality and Social Psychology*, 304-324.

Hayes, L. M. (n.d.). *Lisa M. Hayes > Quotes > Quotable Quote*. Retrieved from GoodReads: https://www.goodreads.com/quotes/655867-be-careful-how-you-are-talking-to-yourself-because-you

Helmstetter, D. S. (2017). *What to Say When You Talk to Your Self*. New York: Gallery Books.

Selk, J. (2009). *10-Minute Toughness*. New York: McGraw Hill.

Spalakoglu, Y. (2019, September 7). *Can We Ever Stop Thinking?* Retrieved from Lives Science: https://www.livescience.com/can-you-ever-stop-thinking.html

University of California. (2019, September 12). *Your Brain is Wired for Negative Thoughts. Here's How to Change It.* Retrieved from YouTube: https://www.youtube.com/watch?v=3ThUrVXz9j0

Chapter 9: Preparation

MacKay, H. (2015, December 20). *Preparation is essentail for achieving success.* Retrieved from Star Tribune: https://www.startribune.com/preparation-is-essential-for-achieving-success/362992721/

Chapter 10: Reviewing Performance

Herbert, B. (n.d.). *Brian Herbert > Quotes > Quotable Quote.* Retrieved from goodreads: https://www.goodreads.com/quotes/670952-the-capacity-to-learn-is-a-gift-the-ability-to

Chapter 11: Closings

Bryant, K. (n.d.). *Kobe Bryant > Quotes > Quotable Quote .* Retrieved from goodreads: https://www.goodreads.com/quotes/10646581-the-most-important-thing-is-to-try-and-inspire-people

ABOUT THE AUTHOR

Jeff grew up in Rochester, MN playing tennis and basketball. He went on to play collegiate tennis at Saint John's University. He coached multiple years of high school tennis and was a club teaching professional for over a decade. Jeff is also a former NCAA men's and women's basketball coach, along with coaching six years of boy's high school basketball. While coaching basketball in Arkansas, he received his Master of Science in Kinesiology and Coaching. After anxiety forced him to step away from coaching basketball, Jeff dedicated his time to learning how to control the mental game. Now he commits his time to helping athletes, teams, and organizations do the same and silence their Inner Rivals and quiet the negativity within.

Looking for a great speaker to take you or your organization to the next level? Reach out to Jeff at:

Jeff@Inner-Rival.com
www.Inner-Rival.com
instagram.com/inner.rival/
facebook.com/InnerRival1

Made in United States
Orlando, FL
16 January 2023

28738484R00117